# BUILD
# YOUR OWN
# GREENHOUSE

CHARLES D. NEAL

# BUILD YOUR OWN GREENHOUSE

## How to Construct, Equip, and Maintain It

CHILTON BOOK COMPANY
Radnor, Pennsylvania

Copyright © 1975 by Charles D. Neal
First Edition     *All Rights Reserved*

Published in Radnor, Pa., by Chilton Book Company
and simultaneously in Don Mills, Ont., Canada,
by Thomas Nelson & Sons, Ltd.

*Designed by Anne Churchman*

Manufactured in the United States of America

*Library of Congress Cataloging in Publication Data*

Neal, Charles D.
  Build your own greenhouse.

  Includes index.
  1. Greenhouses—Design and construction.
I. Title.
SB416.N4        690.8'9        75-5529
ISBN 0-8019-5968-3

Chapter I, Figures 5 and 6, photos of Prefabricated Home Greenhouses (Sun-Glory™, Tropic™) by Sturdi-Built, courtesy of Sturdi-Built Manufacturing Company, Portland, Oregon.
Chapter II, Figure 2, photo of a greenhouse designed and manufactured by Roper IBG, courtesy of Roper IBG, Deerfield, Illinois.
Chapter VII, Figures 4 and 5, and Chapter VIII, Figures 1, 2, and 5, courtesy of National Greenhouse Company.
All other photographs and drawings by Charles D. Neal, unless otherwise noted.

# Contents

# Acknowledgments

During the writing of this book, I have met many greenhouse gardeners and suppliers and corresponded with many more. Since space limitations don't permit my thanking everyone who offered innovative and creative ideas, I sincerely hope each understands my not listing names. Instead I offer a great big thank you to all concerned.

Special thanks go to Dr. Jerry Coorts, Chairman, Plant Industry Department, Southern Illinois University, Carbondale, for his interest, constructive criticism, helpful suggestions, and ideas for the technical sections of the book.

I wish to pay special tribute to Bob Holmes, Greenhouse Superintendent, Southern Illinois University, Carbondale, for many of the practical ideas here.

A good deal of credit goes to Rita Ann Dickemper, who typed the final manuscript. I greatly appreciate her conscientious devotion and industry in meeting assignment deadlines.

Finally, I wish to express my sincere thanks to Benton Arnovitz, Senior Trade Editor of Chilton Book Company, for his encouragement to write the book and for offering many valuable suggestions during the development of the manuscript.

# Foreword

Regardless of where you live, a well-constructed greenhouse can be a gardener's paradise. With a greenhouse you can get a great deal of satisfaction by raising the kinds of plants you enjoy most. And the plants may be native to any part of the world, each growing thing a marvel of beauty in itself. Some plants may be nurtured into full bloom from seedlings, cuttings, and bulbs you've started yourself, while others may be tropical in nature, although you may live in the far north. Then, too, what more pleasing way to have vegetables and herbs on the family table than by raising them in your own greenhouse?

The purpose of this book is twofold. First, I have provided information on building, equipping, and maintaining a greenhouse to meet the gardener's needs, whether it is a window greenhouse for an apartment in a city or whether it is a full-scale greenhouse for a large acreage in a rural setting. In short, I have included a model for every kind of greenhouse gardener with each model designed to make the work both profitable and enjoyable. Second, here is information for the long-standing greenhouse owner who is interested in maintaining his greenhouse and improving it with up-to-date equipment.

In Part I I have explained how to equip and maintain greenhouses. While reading this section, it will help if you'll make notes of the things required for the specific kind of greenhouse gardening you want. Part II gives an easy to follow, step-by-step set of directions on how to build several greenhouse models. I suggest that you construct the basic model you want, then incorporate the items from the notes you gleaned from Part I.

Since I do not intend this to be a technical building trades textbook, actual construction skills are explained just as far as necessary to do the job at hand. And, I have tried to explain the necessary techniques in plain English as well as to illustrate them pictorially in simplified fashion. While written for the layman, I have tried to make the instructions complete enough so that you can do the job like a pro.

Although lists of materials are given for each greenhouse model, no estimates of costs are included. As prices of materials vary from time to time and location to location, you will want up-to-date costs which are had better by requesting suppliers in your area to submit bids from the list of materials you have selected.

Since construction techniques and quality vary, and the availability of many materials fluctuates, I recommend that the purchaser follow the manufacturer's instructions carefully whenever directions accompany merchandise. Most manufacturers will honor their warranties only if the products are assembled and used as recommended. Although I mention certain manufacturers of greenhouse supplies and some products by their trade names, neither I nor the publisher necessarily imply any endorsements or make any guarantee of satisfaction. Here I suggest both warranty and end use be understood by the purchaser and the supplier at the time of actual purchase.

# I

# Greenhouse Essentials

# I

# The Greenhouse Scene

Growing plants inside a greenhouse is fast becoming one of the most popular forms of gardening. High schools and colleges use them; professional gardeners use them; and many tens of thousands of homeowners use them for growing everything from begonias to nutritious vegetables.

To many amateurs, however, gardening in a greenhouse is a completely new experience. Overtaken with visions of an abundance of tropical plants or having at their disposal hundreds of different flowers from all parts of the world, most amateurs stock up on a multitude of species only to find that a simple greenhouse which provides protection merely from the extremes of hot and cold does not always bring satisfactory results.

## PLANT GROWTH REQUIRES FOUR CONDITIONS

Limiting conditions, such as controlled temperature and humidity, are extremely important. A proper balance of heat, light, water, and air are the four conditions essential to an ideal greenhouse climate.

*1-1. This greenhouse serves the people of St. Louis today just as it did when built in 1935.*

3

## GEOGRAPHY MADE TO ORDER

A greenhouse gardener can duplicate the conditions of a tropical forest, a desert floor, an orchard, a mountainside garden, or a vineyard, if he has a proper site, good structural design, and a proper balance of heat, light, water, and air containing the right amount of humidity. Duplicating the interesting and fascinating life found in each of these ecological areas is an accomplishment possible only through the proper use of a greenhouse. Tasty vegetables during the winter, cut flowers any season, tropical plants during snowstorms—these are only a few of the fascinating possibilities. However, most experienced greenhouse gardeners concentrate on one kind of plant, such as orchids, cacti, or mums and then add other plants requiring similar growing conditions. If a special plant schedule was not followed, they would most likely wind up with a conglomeration of all kinds of plants and have no space left, for example, to start annual flowers for the family garden.

## PLANT SUBJECTS

To grow plants native to a particular geographical area successfully depends upon the selection of one of three climatic types with reference to heat and humidity; namely, cool, warm, and tropical. The following table clarifies each of the three types:

| Climatic Type | Night Temperature Range | Degree of Humidity | Examples of Suitable Plants |
|---|---|---|---|
| Cool | 50° | Fairly humid | Aster, carnation |
| Warm | 60° | Moderately humid | Chrysanthemum, roses, snapdragon |
| Tropical | 70° | Very humid | African violet, gloxinia |

By partitioning the greenhouse, it is possible to have two or even all three types operating at the same time. When space becomes cramped, an additional span can be constructed parallel to the original structure. In this way one of the original walls serves as a divider as well as a single wall for both greenhouses, considerably reducing the cost of the second unit.

## STRUCTURE

Generally, plant growth is roughly proportional to the light intensity it receives. Therefore, it is essential to design a greenhouse which will have as much light as possible. A rule of thumb is to construct a greenhouse which has the least amount of opaque top and wall structure (wood, metal, or a combination of both) as practical. This permits a maximum amount of light to enter while at the same time producing a minimum amount of shadow. The top and wall structure need only be structurally sound enough to take the weight of the covering (glass, plexiglass, fiberglass, or plastic) and accumulated snow and ice if this is a problem in your area plus the strain of the severest wind experienced in your locality.

For many years only wood was used as the framework. Now, metal and wood or a combination of both are used. Wood framing must be proportioned wider and thicker than one of metal to provide equal strength per foot run. Because wood has less heat conduction than metal, wood framing loses less heat. On the other hand, because metal framing is slimmer, it admits more light and creates fewer shadows. Maintenance costs with metal framing are lower than those with wood framing.

## CRITERIA GOVERNING LIGHT ABSORPTION

The amount of light absorption is an important quality to consider in selecting the covering for your greenhouse roof and sidewalls.

1. For years, glass was the only material used to cover greenhouse framework. In fact, glass covering is so traditional that in England a greenhouse is frequently referred to as a glasshouse. Not necessarily so today. Plexiglass, fiberglass, and plastic are also widely used as coverings. Although glass is subject to both shattering and breakage by hail and other causes, some authorities recommend it, claiming it has the highest degree of transparency of all three materials. This is disputed by other authorities. For instance, some specialists claim that nylon fiberglass transmits 92 percent of light, while

glass transmits 89 percent. (Note: Use only clear, transparent, or translucent grades of fiberglass. Also use top grades of fiberglass; lower grades, which are relatively inexpensive, may become discolored with age.) These same specialists also claim that glass loses 89 percent of heat by transmission, while nylon fiberglass loses 67 percent. Personally, I favor nylon fiberglass as a covering because it is shatter-proof, hailproof, and easy to keep clean.

Plastic is not in the same league as either glass or fiberglass when it comes to selecting a quality covering. Generally, plastic is acceptable when you need an inexpensive covering. For instance, a greenhouseman operating on a limited budget might cover a cheap structure with plastic until he can afford a better greenhouse. Actually, such planning has a certain advantage. It gives the gardener an opportunity to try out a particular management plan until he is able to build the kind of structure best suited for his gardening requirements. And, there is another advantage. Sometimes the greenhouse gardener runs out of room yet has more planting to do. In this case a plastic model will serve the purpose, and it is inexpensive and easy to construct.

2.   The slope or rake of the roof is also an important part of construction. Too steep a rake creates a mirror effect, reflecting the light rather than transmitting it to the plants.

3.   Direction is another important detail to consider. All things being equal, a north-south orientation is usually best for greenhouses up to about 8 feet by 16 feet that are mainly used during the summer. I recommend an east-west position for larger greenhouses, especially those used throughout the year. To minimize loss of the sun's energy, most greenhouses built up to 25 feet in width have a pitch of 32 degrees. Roofs having less pitch are unsatisfactory, especially in cold climates, because snow does not clear from them well, and they are likely to leak.

4.   Closely related to light transmission is heat transmission. Incidentally, heat and temperature are not synonymous. They are entirely different. Heat is a form of energy within a substance, causing its molecules to move rapidly. Heat is measured in British thermal units (BTUs). Temperature is the measurement of the "coldness" or "warmth" of an object. Almost everyone knows that when the rays from the sun strike the greenhouse covering, heat energy is transmitted to the plants, causing a warming effect. Actually, these rays are ultraviolet or short-wave radiation waves. Remember the colors of the rainbow, red, orange, yellow, green, blue, and violet, forming part of the spectrum? Ultraviolet waves are beyond the violet end of these colors; they are invisible. Ultraviolet is an effective germ killer, too. Objects struck by the ultraviolet waves release heat in the form of infrared or long-wave radiation. These waves are beyond the red end of the spectrum and are also invisible. Since glass, fiberglass, or plastic transmit infrared poorly, most of the heat is retained inside the greenhouse, increasing the total heating effect.

5.   Greenhouse design is an important consideration. Should all walls and roof materials transmit light, or should they consist of a masonry or wood base? This is equally important whether you require a mini-greenhouse constructed within a window of your home or a sophisticated model that has little resemblance to the shape of a traditional greenhouse.

Because of increased energy costs, many gardeners are cutting heating bills by double glazing or insulating their greenhouse roofs and side walls. Instructions are included for insulating the greenhouse models in Part II of this book. Some greenhouse manufacturers are now offering prefabricated insulated greenhouses for sale.

## DESIGN

Greenhouses are constructed in a variety of models, each to serve a specific gardening program. The following models give a general idea of why certain types are built:

**I-2.**   The span roof wall model is designed on the lines of a traditional greenhouse. This model is ideal for the gardener who specializes in raising potted plants on benches. More versatility is afforded by building benches in removable sections, thereby allowing the use of ground beds, too. Masonry or wood walls will lower heating costs somewhat.

**I-3.**   The span roof model, with transparent covering to the ground, for example, is desirable for raising chrysanthemums and tomatoes. This model is ideal for double tier arrangement of benches. Pot plants can occupy the benches, while ferns, lettuce, or cuttings are located underneath. When

I-2

watering, drip from the benches must not be allowed to fall on the plants underneath.

**I-4.** The lean-to model originated with a homeowner who wanted to grow vines and other plants along the south wall of his home. Now it serves the gardener who lacks the space needed for a span-type model but who wants something larger than a mini-greenhouse.

I-3

I-5

I-4

**I-5.** The Dutch-span model, with its span roof and sloping sides that lean toward the ridge of the roof, is in keeping, of course, with Dutch style architecture. The design has special eye appeal for some gardeners. But there is one disadvantage if

*I-7*

you expect to have tall plants, for the margin of space adjoining the walls then becomes unusable.

These are positioned in place to form the side walls; they and the front walls (usually frames of wood)

*I-6*

*I-8*

**I-6.** The unique, sophisticated models are a far cry, in many cases, from what most gardeners refer to as traditional. Generally, they are designed in a number of shapes and sizes, yet provide for under-bench floor gardening, pots on the benches, and hanging baskets overhead. These models offer the ultimate in greenhouse design with this total landscape plan.

**I-7.** Plastic models generally consist of galvanized steel pipes shaped into the form of arches.

are covered with plastic. Sizes vary from full-size to mini-size portables. Of course, plastic is used also over wood structures by some gardeners.

**I-8.** Hotbed or cold frame models are adequate for the gardener who wants only an early crop of garden edibles, such as radishes or lettuce. Either one may be as small as a single frame or as large as a series of frames, sometimes numbering into the dozens. Construction of a hotbed or a cold frame are identical—with the exception of a heating unit for the hotbed. Generally, the frames are of wood or masonry, sloping toward the path of the sun and free from unwanted shade. Removable standard glass sash usually covers the frame. However, plastic films fastened to wood frames are cheaper and provide the required amount of insulation for proper plant growth.

## TYPICAL GREENHOUSE OPERATIONS

Greenhouse gardening is well suited for numerous operations. Some gardeners prefer a part-time operation where they can develop a hobby and perhaps sell garden products to the neighbors to defray expenses; other gardeners prefer a small-scale operation where they have an opportunity to learn the business from the ground up: gardening, advertising, and selling—and, as the business grows, to develop it into a highly profitable enterprise; still other gardeners, either from past experience or by sheer determination, prefer a large-scale operation from the beginning, the gross can range from twenty to seventy-five thousand dollars annually.

Then there is the individual with vision, such as Roger Wohrle in northern New Jersey whose living in a green summerworld all year inspires others to think of greenhouses rather differently. His life style combines his home with an automatically ventilated greenhouse—a fish pond and a swimming pool are included. He basks in summer weather all year, gardens whenever the urge strikes, and uses the swimming pool any time during the year simply by keeping the main thermostat at 68 degrees. Since the swimming pool is heated separately, its temperature is kept at 80 degrees. Since the fish pond and the swimming pool are inside the greenhouse, no humidifier is required to maintain a constant, healthful 50-60 percent humidity.

In short, the range of greenhouse gardening is total, as I have tried to indicate in this work. The following table runs the gamut, from the model greenhouse for the person who wishes to garden as a hobby to the businessman who is self-employed. I'd like to point out that greenhouse gardening as a business can offer unlimited opportunities for expansion and development, as well as providing a healthy atmosphere to work in: no bosses, no commuting, and beautiful surroundings—what fringe benefits! A complete treatise on the subject is impractical. I have tried here to present a general guide or "thought provoker," covering some of the present-day types of greenhouse operations.

## LANDSCAPING YOUR GREENHOUSE

There is no justification for constructing a greenhouse "just any old place" that happens to be conducive to plant growth. Once several likely locations are spotted, determine which site will best fit into your present and future landscaping plans. Like your home, your greenhouse deserves the most attractive setting you can give it.

**I-9.** Desirable site locations can be improved by giving thought to landscaping the greenhouse, as evidenced by these "before" and "after" pictures. Consider walks and driveways not only for accessibility but also in keeping with the preservation of natural resources, such as trees, turf, rock out-

*I-9a*

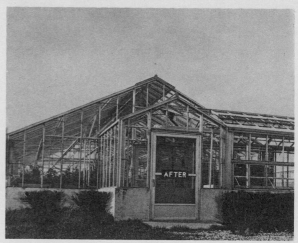

*I-9b*

TYPICAL METHODS OF GREENHOUSE OPERATIONS

| Classification | Greenhouse requirements | Purpose | Supplemental buildings |
| --- | --- | --- | --- |
| Hobby gardener | Small greenhouse, size to suit kinds of plants and amount of involvement planned. | 1. To provide vegetables and herbs for the family table. 2. To grow plants in advance to setting them out in the garden or field during the spring and summer. 3. To test possibilities for going "full-time" in one of the following greenhouse classifications. | None |
| Roadside greenhouse store Operator | Small to large greenhouse, depending upon volume of business anticipated. | 1. To attract attention of passersby. 2. To provide facilities for display of wares and floor area for making sales. 3. To provide storage for blooming plants and flowers until sold. | 1. Greenhouse store with wide glass or plexiglass frames and high eaves, both to serve as "traffic stoppers." 2. Stands with stepped-up benches, inside and outside the store, to display vegetables and other materials offered for sale. |
| Mail-order business | Greenhouse design and size suitable for either part- or full-time with respect to amount of business anticipated. | To attract customers by advertising in garden pages of newspapers, garden magazines, and through direct mailing to people engaged in gardening. | 1. None for part-time work, since space in basement or garage can serve as a combination office and shipping room. 2. Full-time business requires floor space large enough to handle incoming and outgoing mail, packaging and shipping of plant products. |
| Wholesale grocer | Full-time operation calls for a minimum of 12,000 square feet of greenhouse space. | To specialize in growing one or two crops for sale through wholesale commission houses or direct to retail florists. | None, unless operation of a local retail business on the side is anticipated. Then a store building is required, size to suit, for meeting customer demands. |
| Vegetable specialist | Full-time operation requires a minimum of one acre of greenhouse area. | 1. To supply cucumbers, tomatoes, radishes, and lettuce the year around. 2. To produce other less profitable vegetables as demand for them and time and space, is available. | None, other than a garage or shed for storing a delivery truck if wholesaling is your business. Retail business, of course, requires a small store building, size to suit customer traffic. |
| Propagation plant specialist | Small to large greenhouse, size to suit volume of business anticipated. | To raise flowers and other plants from seeds, selling them as young stock in 2-inch flats, pots, or as rooted cuttings. | None, unless your operation calls for a steam or hot water heating system to house in a small shed or lean-to attached to the greenhouse. |
| Greenhouse operator with a "new look" | For complete "new look," greenhouse should contain at least 35' x 80' of floor area to house swimming pool, patio, dining area, fish pond, pathways, fireplaces, and plants, such as aerial roots of the cissus sicyoides vines, house plants, trees, shrubs, and other favorite personal plants. | To provide a combination home and greenhouse for year-round gardening as well as swimming any season of the year in a tropical pool. | Cabin attached to greenhouse with a minimum of 400 square feet of floor space for kitchen facilities, a bathroom, and a small nook for a hot water or steam boiler. A small shed or lean-to for cabana and a separate heating and filtering system for the swimming pool. |

9

croppings, and brooks and streams—if you have them. Of course, geographical location and climate will largely determine the nature of the plants selected—one can do little to change the outdoor geography. Make a landscape plan, even if you require the help of a specialist. Such a plan takes the happenstance out of landscaping. As a result, your home, greenhouse, plants, driveways, and walks will all be in harmony, creating and preserving the beauty in its natural splendor. At the same time, all within your property boundry will remain functional.

# II

# Preliminary Planning

Greenhouses were once constructed purely from the standpoint of growing plants. In many cases, this is still true today. On the other hand, a number of gardeners build greenhouses with an eye for aesthetics, without sacrificing any of the conditions necessary for growing quality plants. Such gardeners like to have a greenhouse where friends can meet, sit in comfortable chairs, and enjoy nature's beauty in all her splendor.

The secret of building a greenhouse to meet your objectives is planning. With forethought the structure can meet all your requirements and at the same time display your personal tastes. To avoid pitfalls that might go undetected during the construction stage, spend plenty of time in initial planning. Changes are both expensive and time-consuming once the greenhouse is completed.

No two greenhouse gardeners are exactly alike. Therefore, it follows, if the objectives of each are to be realized, every greenhouse will be different. The models described in Part II of this book have been selected for their almost universal appeal, so choose the one that comes closest to meeting your requirements, then modify it to your individual needs. Planning tips, general construction practices, and equipment and furnishing possibilities are discussed in the following pages through Chapter IX.

## ZONING ORDINANCES

Zoning ordinances are the legal rules and regulations by which an entire community or sections of it are governed and the nature of their growth controlled. Basically, restrictions are intended to be a genuine protection. Therefore, theoretically, all of them should be designed to protect property owners. Nevertheless, control in the hands of governmental amateurs can result in zoning *against* instead of zoning *for*. One of the first orders of planning is to be certain that a greenhouse, lean-to or free-style, is permitted on your property.

## BUILDING CODES

Another important area to investigate before construction is a building code. Most rural areas and many small towns do not have building codes. Those that do may not have salaried building inspectors, and frequently the code is old-fashioned or out of date. Usually, such communities depend upon the services of volunteers, and they are compensated with a percentage of the building permit fees. In such places, as long as the fee is paid, almost any kind of construction is permitted. If your community has a building code, check two basic requirements: a performance code and a specification code.

1. A *performance code* defines specified performance criteria, regardless of the materials used. Generally, it allows design choice and freedom in using regulation building materials. 2. A *specification code* generally defines the kinds of materials to use. One criticism of such a code is that it can be made-to-order for unscrupulous building suppliers and contractors.

## DEED COVENANTS

Deed covenants are yet further regulations to investigate before building. They are intended to perpetuate the wishes and desires of a previous owner. Generally, such an owner puts his demands in all forthcoming deeds when he subdivides large property. The requirements of zoning ordinances and building codes can be mere child's play compared to rigid and complex deed covenants. On the other hand, a "shady" developer may find that many of his lots are not selling. He removes the deed covenants from all future deeds, allowing the purchasers complete freedom to build. By the time those purchasers having deed covenants bring suit against the developer, they find his land corporation dissolved, which means they have no one to sue. One final comment, deed covenants cannot be superseded by zoning ordinances or building codes.

## LOCATION

Now that you have resolved the applicable zoning ordinances, building codes, and deed covenants, select the best location possible for your greenhouse. Basically, choose the location with respect to prime overall use of your entire property. Sometimes, however, the lot size is such that your only choice is to attach the greenhouse directly to the house or to locate a free-standing model on the only vacant space large enough to accommodate it. Fortunately, most locations generally allow for the ultimate in growing conditions.

Consider these six guidelines while planning your site:

1. Availability of maximum sunlight. Many gardeners prefer a north-south direction—each side of the greenhouse then receives the maximum amount of sunlight. Anticipate shadows cast by tall buildings or trees, those in place or to come. Even those located 60-70 feet away may shade during winter when the sun is low, either in early morning or late afternoon. Sometimes tall deciduous trees to the west can be a blessing in disguise by actually reducing intense afternoon sunlight during the summer yet allowing light to filter through the leafless limbs during the winter.

**II-1.** At other times, trees, especially the older ones, become a real hazard—as shown in the picture. During a mild thunderstorm this tree came

tumbling down. A few feet closer and this greenhouse would have been a total loss. Evergreens, on the other hand, block out sunlight the year round, unless space is kept between them. Sometimes obnoxious trees and buildings are located on adjoining properties, one can do little to eliminate such problems. If this is your concern, take comfort in the fact that three to six hours of sunlight each day will give reasonable success with most plants. If you think you still lack sufficient light, plan to supplement with artificial lighting. The procedure is explained in Chapter VI.

2. Direction and force of prevailing winds. Try to locate the greenhouse where it is not subjected to severe blasts of prevailing winds. Such a location may trap sun in summer, but in late fall, winter, and early spring it can vastly increase the cost of heating. Wind speed can be reduced by planting or building a proper windbreak. Use a slat-type fence or a hedge planted about 15 feet away from the side of the greenhouse. Here the secret is to stay away from dense plants or a solid fence, for a solid windbreak made either of wood or of dense foliage actually increases the wind speed as it is forced over the top, thus developing a more cooling action across the greenhouse covering than if the windbreak were not there.

If you must build in a low area facing slopes bringing in cold air during the winter, a properly built windbreak will accomplish two purposes. First, it will reduce the speed of wind during the winter. Second, it will circulate hot air during the summer, keeping the temperatures at a more desirable level.

3. Drainage, both surface and underground. Select a well-drained location. If necessary, add soil fill so that rainwater will drain away from the greenhouse. To aid underground drainage, if this is a problem, plan to lay 4-inch perforated, plastic pipes to carry away excessive underground water. If you live in an area controlled by a building code, be sure pipes drain into the storm sewer, if one is available.

4. General convenience. If possible choose a site convenient to incoming and outgoing traffic. There is nothing more exasperating or harder on the back, to say nothing of wasted time, than to carry supplies a good distance from the truck to the greenhouse or getting the plant products from the greenhouse to the truck. If the problem exists, a short driveway designed during the planning stage generally does the trick. Also, give *con-*

II-1

II-2

*venience* due consideration in traveling between house and greenhouse. Even if the distance is short, a sidewalk connecting the two is usually worth every cent of the cost.

5.   Sources of water, electricity, and fuel for heating if required. Another important aspect of planning is to understand where access to water, electricity, and heating fuel will be, if electricity will not be the means of heating. If pipes and electric wires are required underground, now is the time to think about their routes and to make certain that there will be no interference during installation.

6.   Appearance or blending into the total landscape scene. Last but by no means least, plan to fit the greenhouse on your lot in such a way that it blends in with your home and the surrounding landscaping. Some gardeners carry the house foundation plan to the greenhouse. For example, if a brick foundation is used on the house, the same type of bricks are used on the greenhouse foundation. Other gardeners use contrasting colors and material, when feasible. Still other gardeners toy around with various creative ideas, developing a landscaped area, including the greenhouse, identifying themselves as the creators.

**II-2.**   Perhaps you can't meet all of the guidelines 100 percent for locating your greenhouse; not many gardeners can. But surely, greenhouses located on city terraces and rooftops, as evidenced in the picture, attest that there are many successful gardeners who didn't back down just because they couldn't meet all the desirable location criteria. In short, you will want to choose the optimum location with respect to your total landscaping plan, then use that site the best way you can, making adaptations as necessary.

### FIRMING YOUR PLANS

The complexity of building a greenhouse depends upon its size and the number and kinds of fixtures and equipment needed to accomplish the gardening goals you have in mind. Regardless of whether you're considering a simple, economy model or an elaborate professional type, before making firm plans, answer the following questions:

a.  Exactly what kinds of plants will be grown?

b.  How many square feet of growing space is required?

c.  How many square feet are required for fixtures and equipment if they cannot be located below or above the growing areas?

d.  How many square feet do you want to give to growing benches?

e.  Do you plan to have furnishings, such as settees, tables, chairs, and etc.? If so, how many square feet of floor space is required?

f.  If you plan a work table inside the greenhouse proper, how much area do you need?

g.  What is the area of walkways, and what do you have in mind for the material?

h.  Is there a possibility of changes in the operation in the near future? If so, what kind of changes? What will be required in addition to what you are now planning?

i.  Do you plan to sell everything you raise? If so, what about plants producing marginal profits? Would it be more profitable to purchase such produce from other gardeners, using that part of the greenhouse for growing more profitable items?

j.  Do you plan to expand in future years? If so, it is wise to plan for that expansion now, even though it doesn't go beyond the paper and pencil stage for some time to come.

### MAKING A LAYOUT

Now that your needs are defined, you are ready to make a tentative layout. Using answers from the questions above, begin by drawing the perimeter of your total floor space on a sheet of black paper, letting ¼ inch represent one foot of floor space. Using filing cards, cut and label scale templates ( ¼ inch represents one foot) for benches, floor growing areas, walks, each fixture and piece of equipment, including furnishings if your plans call for them.

Placing the templates within the greenhouse outline, indicates how everything fits into the given floor space. Do not be surprised if some changes and alterations are in order. Most greenhouse gardeners find this so. Otherwise, there would be little point in spending time in planning.

At this point, make a list of the greenhouse materials, fixtures, equipment, and furnishing. Then secure estimates from your suppliers. In this way you will have a good idea of the financial requirements before you even drive a nail.

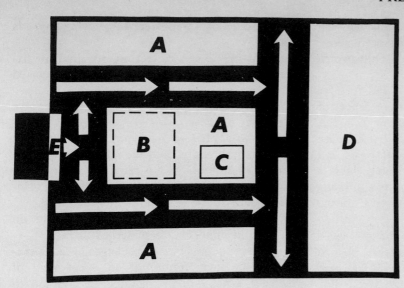

*II-3. Use of scale templates is the best way to find out exactly what floor space is required.*

# III

# Building and Maintaining Your Own Greenhouse

## BUILDING A GREENHOUSE BY YOURSELF

Sooner or later you face up to the question: Can I build a greenhouse by myself? If you are experienced in construction work, you know you can, so skip to the next topic. If this question gives you concern, study the step-by-step procedures accompanying the model of your choice as presented in Part II of this book. The first time through, the various procedures may seem odd. Going over the steps several times gradually brings the whole building procedure into sharper focus. Once you start construction, the information on each step makes more sense when combined with the section that you are actually putting in place. Then, too, if you come to a dead end, your building supplier will be glad to offer suggestions. Generally, there is at least one person working for a supplier who knows material and equipment and how to install or build it. I have actually seen experienced carpenters take off from the job to seek information on a tough construction problem.

Another solution for the inexperienced workman is to trade work with skilled people. Experienced craftsmen do this all the time. If, for instance, an electrician wants to build a greenhouse, he finds other tradesmen who plan on building something—a garage, a house, or a cabin in the woods. The end result is that two or more men agree to exchange an equal number of hours. Not only is each job swiftly completed, but while construction is taking place, there are fewer errors made, for where one worker doesn't understand a particular job, another does. What is good enough for the craftsman is good enough for the novice. In addition, as long as no one receives money in payment for services, a cooperative building program like this generally has the blessing of the local building trades unions.

One further suggestion. Whether you do *all* of the work or have help, don't rush! This can only result in mistakes and discouragements long before the project is completed. Rather, divide your main building goal into small goals or steps, doing each completely, whenever possible, before proceeding to the next step.

## PROFESSIONAL HELP

If you are extremely busy and can spend only a minimum amount of time in building the greenhouse, it may be necessary to hire help for some of the work. In this case, try to be around during the day—even if it is only for a few minutes at a time. This can be time well spent in giving instructions and answering questions. This is not to imply that you will try to tell an experienced craftsman how to do his job. Rather, it means making a decision whenever there is a choice and answering questions that are sure to come up from time to time. If you cannot visit the job during working hours, try to leave a telephone number where you can be reached. With the hourly wage for a good craftsman what it is, you can't afford to have him sit around hour after hour waiting for someone to show up to make a decision.

Hiring professional help to build all or even part of the greenhouse runs into money. Prefabricated or precut greenhouses sold by various green-

16

house factories (see partial list in the Appendix) reduce the need for such help. Also they provide a solution for the man who thinks of his hands as having all thumbs and no fingers. Such suppliers claim to allow the purchaser a savings in overall costs because they have a minimum amount of waste in materials. This is true and it can be true for the amateur builder.

For example, the models in this book are designed on the principal of saving materials. One illustration of this: lumber runs in multiples of two feet. Where wood is used as rafters, length is carefully planned so that the only loss is of the short, diagonal blocks left over at each end. This is a point to consider if you modify one of the greenhouse building plans. For instance, don't end up with the true length of a rafter 9' 2". Either change the design to use rafters 9' in length or enlarge the total structure so that you can use rafters 10' long with a minimum amount of waste. The example of 9' rafters assumes that 18' rafters are purchased and cut in two.

## SUITABLE BUILDING MATERIALS

Both aluminum and redwood are highly recommended materials for building the greenhouse framework. Both are durable and require practically no maintenance. Cost difference is generally the basic reason in selecting redwood over aluminum. Some gardeners argue that redwood has more possibilities from an aesthetic point of view than does aluminum. They point out that it can be stained or painted to enhance the beauty of the home without the commercial appearance or metal look, of an aluminum framework. Not so,

claim the proponents of aluminum structures. These specialists argue that if proper lines are used in the design, along with thought to landscaping, there is no commercial look to detract from the nicest of homes. Both groups, as pointed out in Chapter II, agree that aluminum transmits heat faster than wood; if all other factors are equal, this can mean a slightly higher heating bill. These arguments may leave the reader in a quandary, but after he finds out what materials are available to him and decides which of the two he prefers, he won't make a serious mistake whichever one he chooses for the framework. Sometimes however, aesthetics is given a back seat by the gardener who wants either a quickly constructed, supplementary greenhouse to take care of his immediate expansion, or an economy model with either a cheap wood or metal pipe framework.

Glass, plexiglass, fiberglass, and plastic are used, as noted in Chapter I, as greenhouse coverings. Glass is best in most cases, but where hailstorms are a problem, fiberglass or plexiglass offers an advantage. Sometimes gardeners use fiberglass or plexiglass to cover the roof structure and glass to cover the sidewalls. Corrugated fiberglass is not the most attractive material. Where beauty is part of the greenhouse scheme, I recommend plexiglass, shallow ribbed, or flat fiberglass if something other than glass is desired. Plastic is cheap, in its initial cost, to use as a covering, but its short life and poor appearance generally leaves it for the gardener whose prime consideration is economy. The following table indicates some important differences among polyethylene, vinyl film plastics, and fiberglass when they are properly installed in the greenhouse:

#### Differences in Plastic Greenhouse Coverings

| Plastic and Comparative Costs | Available Widths | [1]Suggested Thickness | Lasting Qualities | Comments |
|---|---|---|---|---|
| Polyethylene (regular) | 3-40 feet | [2]4 or 6 mil | 3 months- 1 year | The reason for the short life of polyethylene is that it breaks down rapidly during hot weather, usually first breaking at the folds. An inside layer saves energy and can cut heating costs by 20 percent or more. |

*Table Continued*

**Differences in Plastic Greenhouse Coverings (Continued)**

| Plastic and Comparative Costs | Available Widths | [1]Suggested Thickness | Lasting Qualities | Comments |
|---|---|---|---|---|
| Polyethylene (ultraviolet-treated)<br><br>Only slightly more costly than un-treated polyethylene | 10-40 feet | 4 or 6 mil | 6-14 months | During late summer or fall use ultraviolet-resistant polyethylene over regular polyethylene. |
| Vinyl (PVC) | 4-6 feet (seamed to larger widths) | 8 or 12 mil | 2-4 years | Use only clear or translucent grades of vinyl, being sure it is weatherable. Although vinyl is pliable and contracts and expands with temperature changes, it does become dirty easily. |
| Fiberglass About 25 times cost of polyethylene | 2-4 feet | 5 oz. minimum (Ask for durability guarantee with purchase) | 6-16 years or longer | Although light is diffused, clear grades can be expected to transmit at least 80 percent of visible light. Shading is often unnecessary. Corrugated or flat fiberglass is available in panels 6-12 feet long, glass-sized panes, and rolls. |

[1] 1 mill equals .991 inch
[2] For inside layer, as noted in Chapter XI, 2 or 4 mil is recommended.

## TOOL USAGE AND REQUIREMENTS

Some people grow up believing there is a great mystery about working with simple tools. Perhaps it stems, in part, from bad early experiences with tools—or lack of any experience at all. I know a man, who for several years wanted to build a greenhouse so he would have something to putter in when retirement became a reality. At the last moment he always shied away from getting started simply because he'd decided that he was clumsy. As a youngster, he was never allowed to use his father's tools. Consequently, he resigned himself to believing there was something incredibly difficult about making even the simplest item. With a little encouragement from his neighbors, however, and some prodding from his wife, he started and finished a very attractive greenhouse.

Although craftsmanship combines knowledge of *what* tools to use for *what* particular job with skill of the hands, a novice can quickly begin to teach himself many of the tricks of the trade. When he attempts to push a wood plane against the grain, for example, he'll make a ragged cut. But when he reverses the cut or pushes a good quality plane with the grain, he'll make a smooth cut, providing, of course, the blade is sharp. Here then are two cardinal principles for using tools:

1. Invest in high quality tools; you can no more turn out quality work with cheap tools than a surgeon can perform a skillful operation with a kitchen knife.

2. Keep your tools well sharpened. If you can't do a good job yourself, farm them out to a tool sharpening specialist. And lastly, even expensive and well-sharpened tools must be protected from the weather and rough handling.

Other than a few masonry and electrical tools, most would-be greenhouse builders already have

*III-1. One tool rental firm's charge for an extension ladder is 2½ percent of its retail cost, while it rents a chain saw for 8 percent of its retail price. Costs are based on one day's use and are determined by their depreciation and specialization.*

enough carpentry tools on hand for the job. The types of tools you'll need to do each job are illustrated and their usage explained at the beginning of each project in this book. If you don't already have the common tools you'll require, it's a good idea to buy high quality items. But if you expect never to use them again, once the greenhouse is finished, it's probably better to rent those tools. Very likely there is a tool-renting service in your area. Most greenhouse builders find that it's far better to pay good prices for average tools and to rent specialized tools than it is to spread the tool budget around and end up with a bunch of cheap, ineffective implements.

## THE TIME TO BUILD

When you build depends upon your geographical location, your free time, and your financial circumstances. Just don't let yourself become discouraged. To the greenhouse builder who is experienced, the time factor is not a problem, but the novice may feel that he reaches a point where he is simply marking time. A certain amount of lost motion is inherent in any building project. But keeping faith in yourself and working little by little soon finds the project completed.

If you expect frozen ground to delay an early start in the spring, you may want to excavate and put in the foundation in the fall, and start the framework in early spring.

## ADVANTAGES OF BUILDING A GREENHOUSE YOURSELF

The foremost reason for building a greenhouse yourself is the saving in money. By doing your own work, you can save as much as 60 percent of the total construction cost. You can save even more if you're willing to scrounge around for bargains. During off-seasons, some material suppliers run sales or for a cash payment will reduce the price on certain items. Another advantage in building your own greenhouse is that you get the kind of construction you want. As you progress from foundation to glazing you not only can make changes as necessary, but you can make them with the least amount of additional costs. Nothing is more disastrous for your pocketbook, if the work is being done by professionals, than to request a radical change in part of the completed structure. On the other hand, a desire to change is natural. No matter how carefully one plans, you'll see opportunities for improvements as the building progresses. I have never talked to a greenhouse builder who didn't admit that there were modifications he would make if he were building again. In any case, the more effort one spends in careful planning, particularly if constructing a greenhouse model, the fewer the changes during construction.

Because the skills required for both building and maintaining a greenhouse are closely related, you should read the following sections carefully even if you are now in the process of building.

You can note special parts requiring maintenance and take precautions to construct them as sturdily and free of maintenance as possible.

## MAINTENANCE

Nothing is made to last forever, and greenhouses are no exception. This is not to imply that your greenhouse is destined for destruction within the immediate future. On the contrary, you can expect lifetime service from it, if you will but provide a little care and make minor repairs periodically.

Maintenance is a series of activities following greenhouse construction, but it is also a subject to think about before you build. Ask yourself how much maintenance your greenhouse will require. No one can tell you the exact number of man-hours per year, but you can do something about keeping the time required to a bare minimum by considering the materials, equipment, and furnishings in its make-up.

Some of the factors involving maintenance have been mentioned indirectly in previous topics on various kinds of greenhouse materials. A framework of wood, for example, requires more maintenance than one of aluminum. Because redwood is less likely to rot and is free from insect destruction, it is generally chosen over other woods for the framework. Due to the extreme moisture content inside a greenhouse, aluminum is often chosen over steel. Unless steel is kept well painted, it will rust, whereas aluminum never rusts. Plexiglass or fiberglass is much preferred, especially for roof coverings, because they are less likely to break than glass; on the other hand, glass is cheaper. Polyethylene is still cheaper, but its life expectancy is generally not longer than one or two seasons. Usually, expensive paints require fewer repeat paintings than bargain-priced paints. In short, the factors involving maintenance are contained in the answer to this question: Is the builder more interested in the initial costs than he is in the costs spread out, say, over five to fifteen years? The answer is a guide to selecting a specific type of greenhouse over others, as well as aiding in selecting the equipment and furnishings for the interior.

Greenhouse maintenance consists of five different activities, namely, carpentry, glazing, painting, removing algae, and general.

### Safety Tips

Before beginning either construction on a greenhouse or maintenance on an existing structure, think seriously about safety measures to protect yourself, members of your family, and others who might be working with you against unnecessary accidents. Any insurance agent can tell you that the accident rate is high in all kinds of construction. Some accidents result in death, others result in partial or total disability.

Many lesser accidents result in minor cuts, sprains, broken limbs, and bruises. Not only are they painful, but they lose you many working hours. Every construction workman who is conscious of safety knows that accidents result from carelessness or from putting off till tomorrow what should be done today. For example, planning to repair that loose hammer head tomorrow may result in an accident today. A person who knows he will be involved with construction work should have a tetanus antitoxin inoculation. Booster shots are necessary thereafter. Some local health departments provide free inoculations. The following guidelines should help keep accidents to a minimum.

### Safety Guidelines

*Clothing*

1.   Trousers should not be too long. Cuffs are likely to catch heels, causing falls or tripping. Trousers of the right length, without cuffs, are best.

2.   Shirt or jacket sleeves shouldn't be too long. They should be kept buttoned to prevent them from catching on projecting nails or pieces of projecting framework.

3.   Wear safety shoes as a protection from falling objects. Be sure your shoes have thick soles to protect your feet from nails.

4.   Protective goggles are a must when there is a danger of flying particles, such as occurs when sharpening tools with a grinder.

*Tools*

5.   Keep both hand tools and power tools clean and in good working order.

6.   If you purchase a new, unfamiliar tool,

learn how to use it properly before taking it on the job.

7. Do not use hammers or axes with split or cracked handles or loose heads. Repair them first.

8. Keep chisels, knives, saws, plane blades, and all cutting tools sharp; protect them at all times from unnecessary damage.

9. Check screwdrivers occasionally for loose or broken handles and broken points.

10. Pay particular attention to level-type tools, keeping them in good working order. A pinch on the skin from a poorly working pair of pincers may cause a blister. This in turn could result in blood poisoning if not given proper attention.

11. Be sure ladders are strong and set up properly before use. Ladders with weak or patched side rails or weak or broken rungs should be discarded.

12. Power tools, like cutting-type hand tools, must be kept sharp, properly oiled, and properly cared for.

13. Use power tools only for their intended purpose. Know how to use them and what safety measures are required for each. For instance, never stand directly behind the blade of a table saw when using it. Always stand to the side, thus avoiding being hit—possibly in the eye—by flying lumber if a kickback occurs.

## Electricity

14. Hold a high regard for electricity. Don't join the Famous Last Words Club by showing your friends how much "juice" you can take without its hurting you.

15. When working with power tools or other electrical equipment, including trouble lights, be sure cords (including extension cords) are properly covered, and that both wires and switches are designed to carry the amount of current expected to pass through them.

16. Avoid splicing cords whenever possible and be certain that cords designed for interior use are never used outside.

17. All power tools should be properly grounded or properly designed by the manufacturer to prevent shocking the operator.

18. Never use power tools outside in wet weather or where you must stand or lie down on wet ground. Even if the ground is not puddled in water but only damp, working with power tools under such conditions can make you a number one candidate for the morgue.

19. Never work on an electrical wire by itself or one connected to an electric fixture until you are certain that neither end is connected to power.

20. Avoid working on electrical equipment or electric wires until the circuit of which they are a part has been disconnected by removing its fuse or pulling its circuit breaker.

## Practical Housekeeping

21. Always remove nails from forms and scrap lumber; then stack that wood in place away from the immediate working area.

22. Place scrap materials and rubbish in containers daily to help reduce accident possibilities and to prevent unwanted fires.

23. Keep building materials, such as lumber, concrete blocks, or bricks in neat, well-balanced stacks.

24. Use gloves while handling glass panes; always store the glass in a place safe from breakage.

25. When working above ground level, be sure unused tools are placed on solid footing so they don't fall on you or anyone else.

## First Aid

26. Learn how to administer first aid. A number of volunteer agencies in every community give free lessons.

27. Keep a first-aid kit handy. Make it a part of your greenhouse furnishings.

## Woodworking Suggestions

Sooner or later the greenhouse gardener becomes involved in a certain amount of carpentry: actual construction of the greenhouse and some of its equipment, replacement of wood sections, or remodeling. Although patience is of utmost importance, obviously, this is not all that is necessary to make an amateur's work look like that of a pro. Quite often, a simple technique is the key to giving the job that professional look—however, simple or not, it is unknown to the amateur. Here are twenty woodworking suggestions to help you do the best possible job:

1.   You do not need a full complement of carpentry tools to build a greenhouse. Most lumber dealers will rip wide boards into narrow ones, cut 4 x 8-foot sheets of plywood into smaller pieces, and provide other sawing services for a small fee. For lumber specification sizes as they relate to actual dimensions, see Appendix, Table II.

2.   If you store lumber, keep it in good shape. Badly warped lumber means wasted lumber. Wet lumber has a tendency to warp as well as being hard to work; it also dulls your tools.

3.   For accurate work, use a scriber or a sharp-pointed instrument to mark cutting lines on pieces of wood requiring sawing or planing.

4.   To avoid slightly undersized pieces of wood, saw on the waste side of the line.

5.   If you'll need to make several pieces of the same dimensions, use the first piece as a pattern and, mark it with a "P."

6.   When using a plane, adjust the blade parallel to bottom of plane.

7.   Plane wood parallel to the grain. Otherwise, you chip the wood.

8.   Use full-length strokes when planing. Remove the plane at the end of the piece.

9.   When driving nails, always hold the hammer handle near the end.

10.   To prevent marring your wood and bending nails, place a block of wood under the hammer "target."

11.   Stop drilling when the bit point comes through the underside of wood; turn the board over and finish the job from the other side.

12.   **III-2.** Miter joints are best sawed in a box manufactured for the purpose. If you don't have one, the picture shows how to make one. Nail two 1-inch boards of equal size to a 2-inch board as shown. Measure squaring lines on top edge of each board as far apart as the wood

is wide. Using ends of lines diagonal to each other as points, saw two perpendicular kerfs (see glossary), forming guides later used for sawing boards at a 45° angle. The right angle cut across the miter box to the rear of the 45° cuts is used to cut plastic pipe and to make square cuts on narrow lumber, such as moldings.

13.   You can make rabbet cuts (see glossary) in wood for making greenhouse sash with a set of dado blades and a power saw. If you do not have the dado blades, make two passes over edge of frame member, one for depth, the other for width.

14.   If nails split wood when driving them, first drill a hole slightly smaller than diameter of nail. This is especially helpful when fastening thin pieces of wood together or when nailing close to end of board.

15.   Use a nail set for countersinking finish nails.

*III-3*

16.   **III-3.** Hold boards in vise as shown when nailing miter joints together.

17.   When putting pieces of wood together with screws, drill a hole through the piece through which the screw passes slightly smaller in diameter than that of the plain shank of the screw.

18.   Moist soap placed on the threads of screws makes them turn more easily in the wood. This is also true of nails and is particularly helpful if you are driving them into hardwood.

19.   Fill large holes in wood by inserting and gluing pieces of matching wood.

20.   Small holes and cracks in wood can be filled with a paste made of sawdust and glue. Where the wood is to be finished with paint, use wood putty or glazing compound to fill small holes and cracks.

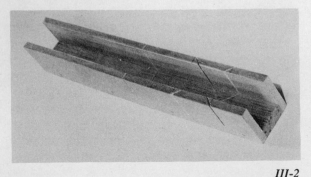

*III-2*

## Replacements

After the greenhouse is in operation for a while, inspect it periodically to observe what kinds of replacement, if any, are needed. Replace rotted or broken pieces of framework with painted, duplicate pieces of wood. Major greenhouse supply houses carry a variety of wooden framework parts rabbeted ready to glaze: roof bars, roof end bars, eave plates, ridge caps, wall bars, side wall bars, gable bars, glazing sill, and many more. However, if you are handy with tools, it is less expensive to cut and rabbet them yourself, using the discarded parts as patterns. Replace broken glass with new panes properly glazed (described in the next section). You may want to replace glass panes with plexiglass for greater durability. However, if you use glass for the replacements, use nothing weaker than double strength.

Film plastics, such as polyethylene and vinyl, have the advantage of low initial costs but considerable maintenance is required with these materials to keep them in good repair. Polyethylene not only has a short life, it also has a tendency to break down rapidly during the summer. While making inspections, pay particular attention to the folded areas. It is here that deterioration first takes place, then it spreads rapidly to other areas. Since polyethylene can be secured in rolls up to 14 feet wide, be sure replacements are made with a minimum number of folds and joints. It is a good idea not to use material thinner than 4 or 6 mils. Of the two thicknesses, 6 mils is the best choice.

Because vinyl has a way of becoming dirty as well as having a short life, it needs replacement often. Always use a clear or translucent grade in replacement.

## Glazing

*Cutting Single Strength and
Double Strength Glass*

If you have never cut a piece of glass, don't give up in despair. Basically, glass cutting is a two shot operation: scoring the surface, then applying pressure along the scored line to form a clean break. Using the following information, practice on a few scrap pieces of glass until the cut is smooth and of even density.

Preparation is most important. Try short cuts

and you are headed for trouble. Here's what you need:

a. Mix equal parts of kerosene and light oil together to half fill a small, clean can. I use a 5-ounce pudding can.

b. Place a piece of indoor-outdoor carpet or a ½-inch layer of newspapers on the working surface.

c. Straightedge with a nonslip bottom. Placing a strip of masking tape on the underneath side of a yardstick or metal ruler serves the purpose well.

d. Wheel type or diamond point cutter. Either one is satisfactory. I use a wheel type and purchase three or four at a time, because some work better than others.

e. One-half-inch dowel, length to suit. Use a plane to flatten bottom side slightly.

*III-4*

**III-4.**   Here's how to make the cut:
Be sure temperature is not below 75° F.
Position glass on padded surface.
Measure to locate start and finish points of cut. Then mark points with a felt marker.
Using marks as guidelines, position straightedge on glass, holding firmly with one hand.
Hold the cutter as shown, between first and second fingers with thumb on underneath side. (Note: Some glass cutters wrap fist around the cutter, with thumb on top of ball end.) Use the grip that is most comfortable. *Caution:* If cutter is held too tightly, you will lose control and place excessive pressure on the glass. Excessive flaking is an indication of improperly held cutter. Ragged cuts indicate the wheel is either frozen or dull.
Dip cutter into can of lubricant. Next make the cut in one even stroke. Never slow the speed near end of cut. Repeating a cut over a scored

line almost always results in a ragged unclean cut, to say nothing of dulling the cutter wheel.

With each hand held on opposite edge of glass, position scored line directly over a dowel. Apply pressure downward on each side of glass at the same time to make a neat cut. To break heavier glass, use ball end of cutter, tapping along score line on opposite side of glass. Remove a narrow strip by applying pressure with your thumb and index fingers only where the score line begins. *Caution:* Glass has a property known to the pros as healing. Scored lines will heal within two minutes, so make the break immediately following scoring.

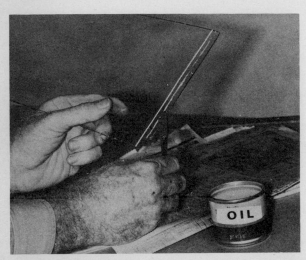

III-5

**III-5.**   Break extremely narrow pieces of glass by using one of the notches in the cutter for applying pressure during the cut. Here a used piece of glass serves as well as a new piece after the chipped edges were removed.

### Cutting Plexiglass

Sometimes holes are required in plexiglass. These are easily made with an electric drill and a high-speed drill bit, size to suit.

There are two ways to cut plexiglass. One way is to use a plastic cutting tool, which can be purchased from your local glass store. Since the tool makes a minute trench when used, you can repeat the cutting operation until the plexiglass is completely cut. Another way to cut plexiglass is to use a saw with fine teeth. I use a saber saw fitted with a blade consisting of 10 teeth per inch. Some

professionals use bandsaws. Even a handsaw will do, but it soon runs into hard work.

### Installing The Panes

III-6

**III-6.**   When you discover a broken pane, replace it as soon as possible. Begin by removing all the old putty. Clean the bar tongues of their weathered condition with a wire brush. Follow up with a coat of good quality paint. (Note: unpainted wood bar tongues absorb the oils from the putty and cause it to crack and break away from its position.) When the paint is dry, have available a glazing chisel, glazing points, putty, and panes cut to size as previously described. Two stepladders and a piece of 2 x 10 make a good scaffold; place this so you can walk up between the roof bars from eave to ridge as you lay in the panes. For a replacement of single panes in one or more frames, use a roof scaffold as described in Figure #16.

Next putty the bars. Once you are on the scaffold, ball some putty in your hand. Then push it into the glass ledge on the bars with your thumbs. As you do so, wipe it in so as to fill the ledge evenly with a V-shaped strip of putty from eave to ridge on both sides of bars, bars excepted. Here only inside ledge requires putty.

**III-7.**   Now a helper is useful to hand you the panes. Press the pane firmly in place so only a thin layer of putty remains underneath it. Actually, the putty should squeeze out from all sides. For a leakproof job, lay the pane right the first

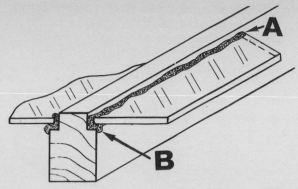

*III-7*

time. Using a putty knife, cut outside putty A level with glass surface. Wait 8–24 hours before cutting inside putty B plumb with bar. Use excess putty, but first mix a little linseed oil with it to retain its flexibility. *Caution:* Do not allow putty to remain on outside surface of pane. Sooner or later it will cause numerous leaks. No matter who advises you otherwise, don't leave any putty on top side of pane.

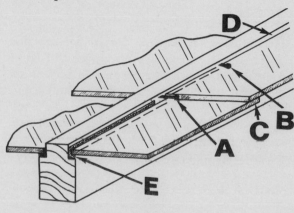

*III-8*

**III-8.** Next hold panes in position by driving in four glazing points for each pane. Using a glazing chisel, drive two points A, one on each side, just below lower edge. This prevents the pane from sliding downward. Then drive two points B about 2 inches up from lower edge of pane, one on each side. Now place and bed next pane in place so that lap is no less than ¼ inch and no greater than ⅜ inch. Do not exceed a ⅜ inch lap. Large laps collect dirt and make for a shoddy job.

Continue right on up the row, laying one pane after another. As you complete a row of panes examine the putty seal before leaving, cutting off any excess putty D. As mentioned previously, cut excess putty E after waiting for it to begin setting

up, usually 8–24 hours. Exactly how long to wait? If some of the putty pulls out from under the panes, it is too soft, and you are in for leaks. There must be a continuous strip of putty from eave to ridge under the glass all along the bar tongues on both sides of each row. (Note: You can secure both glazing chisel and glazing points from your local hardware store or from greenhouse supply houses, such as National Greenhouse Company, Pana, Illinois.)

*Alternate Seals*

Caulking compound, placed in a glazing gun, can be used to provide a weathertight seal between pane and bar tongues.

An alternative is Puttitape (not to be confused with traditional putty) distributed by National Greenhouse Company. Puttitape is believed to have several advantages over caulking compounds. With it there's no bubbling; no putty gun is required; no top painting is necessary; and five steps complete the job. 1. Unwind ribbon of Puttitape, running one continuous length from eave to ridge. If necessary, make splices by lapping tape. 2. Remove strips of paper which tape is laid on. Be sure *not* to remove aluminum backing. 3. Center tape over bar, running roller (also distributed by National Greenhouse Company) over center part, pressing it down on bar tongue. 4. Using roller, work down sides, pressing firmly into corner. 5. Feather-out edges on glass, being sure they stick tight. You'll find the tape tacky and sticking well on a sunny day with a temperature no lower than 70°F.

Sometimes glass panes are unbroken but rain water leaks inside between the edges of the glass and the tongues of the bars. When you have this problem, clean and paint bar tongues as previously described.

If the glass surface has signs of scum, clean it with turpentine or paint thinner. If glazing points are missing, replace them. Then seal with putty or Puttitape as described above.

*Strengthening Wood Joints*

While either doing the maintenance work or constructing a new greenhouse, it is good to provide added strength to some of the wood joints. One way to make framing members more rigid is to coat the joints with a waterproof glue before you fasten them together. I use resorcinol-resin glue because it is waterproof and sets under low pressure at normal air temperatures.

III-9

**III-9.** Another way to reinforce small frames, such as ventilating and sash frames, is to drive a corrugated fastener into each joint.

III-10

**III-10.** Still another reinforcement method is to force a short piece of wooden dowel pin covered in a waterproof glue into a predrilled hole, as illustrated.

III-11a

**III-11.** The pictures show three types of metal

III-11b

III-11c

reinforcements and their use. Most hardware stores carry these in different sizes to suit the job at hand.

**Doors**

Some greenhouse builders and remodelers use doors purchased from a lumberyard. These may be solid, exterior doors, storm doors, or jalousie doors. The latter two provide more glass area to the greenhouse, as well as additional ventilation when required. On the other hand, many greenhouse builders and remodelers make their own doors, primarily because this is inexpensive.

Whether you use a manufactured wood door or make one as described next, the installation, door,

*III-12*

Exterior ¼-inch-thick hardboard, such as Masonite or ¼-inch-thick weatherproof plywood, fastened on one or both sides of frame makes for a more substantial door. Cut sheet to size, then spread resorcinol-resin glue over framework prior to positioning sheet. Then use 1-inch prefinished panel nails spaced about 8 inches apart to give added holding power to the sheet. The materials described for making doors are handled by most lumberyards.

By rabbeting rails A and stiles B, you can permanently fasten a panel of hardboard or plywood in the lower section of the door and make a removable glass sash for the upper section. (Note: See following section for making sash.) Hold sash in place with small tuxon buttons found in any lumberyard or hardware store.

Before painting door two coats of exterior paint, color of your choice, be sure door works freely in door frame, as described later in this chapter. Also, see painting section later in this chapter.

hinges, lock set, and door stop for either, is handled in the same manner.

**III-12.**   Make door frames from 5/4-inch clear stock. Begin by cutting two stiles A 3 inches wide x 6 feet 8 inches long. Next cut middle and lower rails B 5 inches x a length which plus widths of two stiles A equals width of door frame. (Note: Allow ³⁄₁₆ inch for free movement when opening and closing door later.) Now cut top rail C 3 inches x same length as previously cut rails.

Fasten stiles A to rails B with three 3-inch #10 round-head wood screws at joints with the exception of lock location joint. Here use only two screws spaced apart far enough to allow for cutting lock mortise later. Similarly, fasten top end of stiles A to rail C. Here use only two screws for each joint. Prepare stiles A for countersinking screws by drilling holes 1½ inches deep x diameter slightly larger than screw head. (Note: picture shows a screw positioned in hole before tightening.) Following tightening of screws with screwdriver, fill holes either with dowel pins cut flush with edges and coated with waterproof glue or with your favorite brand of wood filler. Then sand edges smooth.

For an inexpensive covering, use 4–6 mil plastic film on both sides of frame held in place with screen molding fastened with 18 gauge x 1-inch wire nails spaced 4 inches apart.

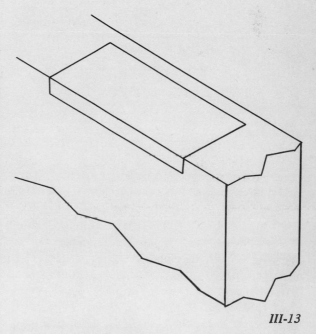

*III-13*

**III-13.**   These steps complete the hanging of a wood door with a pair of half-surface hinges.

Using dimensions of hinge leaf, layout one hinge gain (see glossary) on door jamb 7 inches from top of door frame. Wall studs can be used to double as a door frame. Using a sharp wood chisel, make a vertical cut completely around gain. Be sure to keep flat side of chisel turned out.

**III-14.**   Holding chisel at an angle as you

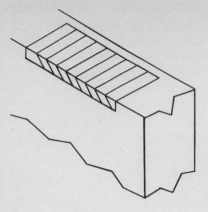

*III-14*

strike sharp blows with a mallet, chip the wood from end to end of gain.

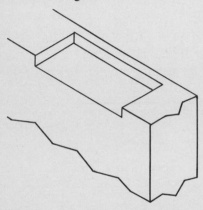

*III-15*

**III-15.**    Working from open side with flat side of chisel down and in a horizontal position, strike chisel lightly with mallet as you remove the chipped material. Next layout second hinge gain on door jamb 11 inches from bottom of door frame. Then remove material as described above.

Study the instructions accompanying the type of door lock you plan to use. Then prepare mortise both on door jamb opposite hinge locations and on door edge, then drill hole for mounting door knobs to spindle. Templates and instructions packed with lock sets make these jobs simple.

With the loose pin up, position hinge in gain mortised in door jamb. Using screws in package fasten in place, ensuring hinge fits tightly against back of gain. Fasten second hinge in the same manner.

Temporarily position door in door frame. Then hold in place with small wood wedges driven between door and door frame. For door to swing freely, height of door frame should be ½ inch more than the height of door, while width of the door frame should be $\frac{3}{16}$ inch more than the door width. If door binds, plane or saw to suit requirements. With door blocked solidly in place, fasten free hinge leaves to door.

Remove blocks and assemble lock set as described on the instruction sheet accompanying package.

Mitering joints, use #4-finishing nails spaced 16 inches apart to fasten door stop in place on sides and top of door frame face. Be sure door rests against stop when closed without door latch binding.

## Sash

Sash in general, as well as hotbed sash complete with glass panes, can be purchased from lumberyards and most greenhouse supply houses. On the other hand, you can make sash to your specifications and fit them with glazing material; this is cheaper. One way is to purchase rabbeted stile and rail stock from greenhouse suppliers. Then cut, assemble, and glaze to your specifications. Alternately, you can make your own rabbeted rails and stiles from 5/4-inch clear stock from your lumberyard. These can be fastened together similarly to fastening door stiles and rails together (described above).

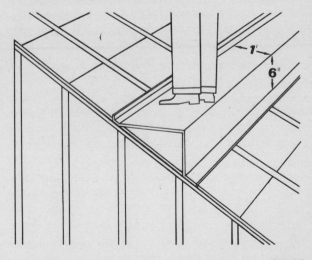

*III-16*

**III-16.**    Fit manufactured aluminum roof scaffold with specially located notches against screws placed permanently in the roof bars; this makes painting and repairing the greenhouse roof a breeze. This is available from major greenhouse suppliers, such as National Greenhouse Company.

Because the wooden framework inside a greenhouse is in constant contact with a high degree of moisture, it usually is subject to scaling and rot. To preserve the wood, thoroughly brush in two undercoats of paint and one finish coat, following a thorough job of removing scaled paint, cleaning the framing materials, and making replacements where rot makes repair impossible. *Caution:* Be sure undercoats and finish coat are designed for exterior use; it is better to use paint especially designed for greenhouses. Since rot begins at the end-grain sections and joints before spreading to other parts, these places should be thoroughly sealed during the undercoating. The best way to ensure proper sealing is to undercoat the individual framework pieces before assembling them. Once the undercoating is completed and the framework assembled, fill all nail and screw holes and wood imperfections that are potential holders of moisture with window glaze compound or caulking compound. I use window glaze compound for filling nail and screw holes and small cracks and caulking compound for filling larger cracks. (Note: Window glaze compound and caulking compound remain elastic to allow for contraction and expansion, whereas putty hardens and as it does, has a tendency to fall out of holes and cracks. Also, it is not advisable to use either window glaze compound or caulking compound prior to undercoating. To do so causes the bare wood to absorb their oils, resulting in hairline cracks between the two different materials.)

Once the framework and glazing are completed, apply the final coat of paint. Some greenhouse builders apply the final coat of paint to the individual pieces instead of waiting until the structure is completed and glazed. This is the easiest way to do the job, but it provides neither as good a finish nor as effective a weather seal. It is important to seal completely with paint the juncture of glass, or any other materials requiring glazing, and framework. Otherwise hairline cracks develop, allowing moisture to form under the paint, which causes paint to blister and scale and wood to rot. As a further precaution against rot, for the framework use wood treated with a nontoxic preservative.

If you look at a number of greenhouses, you will find some that have been painted colors other than white. However, the professional greenhouse gardener generally uses white because it reflects light best. Black, of course, does not reflect light at all.

Because the paint on the greenhouse is subjected to two climates, namely, man-made climate on the inside and nature's climate on the outside, purchasing bargain paints is extremely poor economics. I recommend special greenhouse paint. The kind containing a fungicide is preferable. If your local building supplier does not carry this type of paint, contact one of the greenhouse suppliers listed in the Appendix. *Caution:* Never use paints which emit toxic vapors, especially those containing mercury compounds.

Treat benches and other wood members near or in the ground with a 2 percent copper naphthenate. *Caution:* Never use pentachlorophenol or creosote preservatives in the greenhouse.

Always use a clean brush, large enough to do the job at hand. How large a brush depends upon *how* it feels to you as you stroke it back and forth over the framework. The brush does not necessarily need to be new, but do not use one brush interchangeably for paint and varnish.

*III-17*

*III-17. Rather than wipe brush on side of container so excess paint trickles down outside, run a piece of clothesline wire (bent at each end) through holes made near top of container to serve as a paint wiper (white arrow), allowing excess paint to trickle down inside container.*

If you use a latex paint, clean the brush with soap and water at the end of each painting session. Use paint thinner or turpentine for cleaning the brush of oil-base paint.

Sometimes painted surfaces are in good condition but are simply dirty. Here a washing with a paint cleaner, such as Soilax, usually restores the paint to its former cleanliness. Soilax is a powder which you mix with warm water to remove dirt, grease, and sticky film. You can buy it from most grocery stores. Mix one ounce to the gallon of warm water and clean the surface with a wet sponge. To avoid streaks, work from the bottom up. This is a time-saving cleanser, since no rinsing is required.

If painting is required and the surface is dirty, clean away the soil with a paint cleaner, such as Soilax, before you apply the paint. If the painted surface is in fair condition, a cleaning followed by one coat of quality exterior paint usually gives the appearance of a two-coat job.

Painting is not recommended for greenhouses with aluminum bars and aluminum framework.

### Removing Algae

Algae are simple green plants. Because they manufacture their own food, they are called independent plants. The species found inside the greenhouse have the scientific name of *pleurococcus* or *protococcus*. Since algae require a moist environment in which to multiply, a greenhouse climate is ideally suited for carrying on their life processes. Although this is a natural phenomenon, they become a nuisance.

Many species of green algae (*chlomydomonas, oocystis,* and *euglena*) and bluegreen algae (*oscillatoria* and *arthrospira*) may be found in the greenhouse.

The best method of controlling algae in the greenhouse is through cleanliness. Hosing down the inside of the greenhouse periodically to remove dust particles and spores is beneficial. It should be done on a sunny day so that the greenhouse, as well as any plants present, will dry out by evening. Chemical algaecides are available but may be toxic to some plants should the solution get on their foliage. Roof bars of wood should be kept clean to minimize decay; they should be repainted periodically. This will also contribute to making the greenhouse appear lighter inside.

### General Maintenance

Since repair steps and care in general maintenance are similar to installation steps, see appropriate chapters in this book on plumbing, electricity, heating ventilation, cooling, and humidification.

# IV

# Greenhouse Basics

## LAYING OUT THE GREENHOUSE

The amount of preparation necessary for the layout is determined when you select a specific kind of greenhouse. A walled type, with a house where the wall will be, say, 2½ feet high, made of concrete blocks or poured concrete, requires two construction operations: 1. Pouring the footing; and 2. Constructing the wall on top of the footing. With a transparent greenhouse from ridge-to-ground, a concrete footing with masonry just high enough to clear the ground a few inches may be all that is necessary.

Check the building code, if one exists in your area, to find out if there are regulations governing the construction of a greenhouse, or, in fact, any building separate from your home. For instance, some codes determine the minimum distance *any* building must be set back from a street or road.

*IV-1*

**IV-1.** In addition to a straight, unwarped leveling board, the picture shows tools required for the layout job. See glossary for definition and/or use of each.

1. Tri-square or combination square
2. Handsaw
3. Carpenter's hammer
4. Carpenter's level
5. Steel tape
6. Nylon string
7. Plumb bob
8. Line level

Materials for the layout job are in the following table:

### Layout Materials

| Name | Description |
|---|---|
| Corner stakes | 1 x 2-inch lumber, length to suit |
| Batter boards | 1 x 4-inch lumber 3 feet long |
| Batter-board stakes | 1 x 2-inch lumber about 2 feet long |
| Nails | 6-penny box |

*IV-2*

**IV-2.** On selection of a site after consideration of the important location factors noted—light and shade—drive two corner stakes A and B with their centers the required distance apart, set back at your discretion from some object of reference, such as a street or another building. Now drive a 6-penny box nail into the center of

31

each stake, leave about an inch of nail exposed. Next stretch a cord from nail in stake A to nail in stake B, forming outside edge line of one side of greenhouse.

*IV-3*

**IV-3.** Measure off side BC from base stake B. Drive in temporary base stake C. Then drive a 6-penny box nail part way into center of stake. Stretch nylon cord from B to C. Next be sure corner ABC forms a right angle (90°). Check by measuring off a distance of 8 feet with a steel tape from stake B along line BA. Using a pencil or pen, mark this point on the cord. Next measure off 6 feet from stake B along line BC, marking the point as before. Now, unfasten cord at point C. Then hold cord from this end as you move it back and forth until the distance between the two pencil marks on lines AB and BC are exactly 10 feet apart. Now you are certain angle ABC is a right angle. Reposition stake C and refasten cord. (Note: It's always a good idea to recheck the angle again following the driving of the stake in its final position. You'll need help for this operation.)

*IV-4*

**IV-4.** Measure off sides AD and DC. Drive in temporary base stake D, followed by driving a 6-penny box nail part way into center of stake. Be sure distance DC equals distance AB. Next,

stretch the cord from points C to D to A. Make right angle checks, as described above, on the three corners just established. Further check by measuring the diagonals AC and DB. Both should be of the same length. If they are not the same length, one or more of your corners are not 90°, and rechecking is in order.

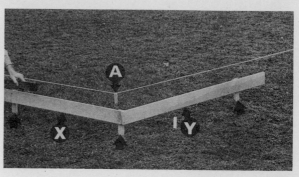

*IV-5*

**IV-5.** The next job is to construct batter boards. Using a hammer, drive in three batter board corner stakes (shown by arrows) near one of the building line corner stakes, such as A in the picture, in the form of a right-angle triangle, one to two feet outside the building lines. Be sure middle stake is in line with two diagonal building line corner stakes and that tops of the three batter board stakes are in the same horizontal plane. Use a carpenter's level positioned on a straight edge for checking. Next, using 6-penny box nails, fasten two 1 x 4-inch x 4-feet batter boards X and Y to batter board stakes. Use a carpenter's level to check that top edges are flush with top of stakes.

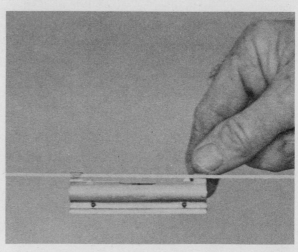

*IV-6*

**IV-6.** Construct batter board stakes and batter boards in the same manner at the three remaining corners. It is necessary to have top edges of *all* batter boards on the same plane. If you don't have access to a transit, use a line level (illustrated) attached to the middle of a nylon cord stretched tight between batter board assemblies, checking two at a time, for constructing three remaining sets of batter boards all on the same horizontal plane as the first set. A line level is accurate enough for the job at hand, providing the cord is kept taut.

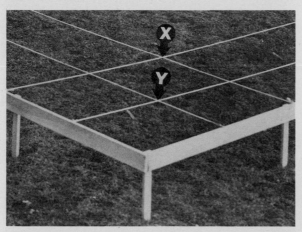

IV-7

**IV-7.** Now you are ready to show the length and width of the outside building lines and the footing dimensions on the batter boards. Begin by stretching a nylon cord, held in place with a 6-penny box nail at each end, over top edges of two batter boards and directly over the building line cord established in Step 4. Using either a plumb bob or a carpenter's level to check, being sure cord over batter boards is directly over building line cord. Then mark line location with a pencil mark on each pair of batter boards. (Note: For more permanent marking, use a hand saw to cut shallow kerfs through pencil mark.) Repeat operation directly over the three other building line cords. Now remove building line cords and stakes (laid out in Step 4). Also, remove building line cords from batter boards. Next locate footing line cords on batter boards. A footing is a level and solid base on which the foundation and wall, if your greenhouse requires one, are built. For example, an 8-inch concrete or concrete block wall requires a footing of 16 inches in width. Generally, footing widths are made twice the widths of the walls. Measuring from building line marks on batter boards, mark footing line locations on

batter boards. Now fasten footing lines X and Y across top edges of batter boards, as illustrated, holding lines in place with 6-penny box nails. Since lines require moving, do not fasten them permanently to batter boards.

## PREPARING AND POURING THE FOOTING

A shovel, plumb bob and cord, level, and carpenter's hammer are the tools required, and leveling pegs are the materials for preparing the footing.

IV-8

**IV-8.** Drop a plumb bob from the footing lines to the ground periodically, marking footing locations with a small stake or a shallow cut made in the ground with a shovel or hatchet. (Note: The plumb bob illustrated is a combination plumb bob and chalk line.)

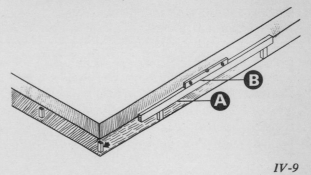

IV-9

**IV-9.** Remove inside footing cords from batter boards. Then, using markings on the ground as guide marks, use a shovel to dig a trench below the frost line. This prevents frost from getting under the footing later, to throw the greenhouse out of plumb. If frost is not a problem in your area, top of footing need be only a few inches below top of ground. *Caution:* For full carrying capacity, trench must have a square bottom. To assure a fairly level bottom, check with a guide stick periodically between outside footing cord and bottom of trench as you dig. Make a guide stick from a scrap piece of wood It should be as long as the frost line is deep, plus distance from ground level—where you begin digging—up to outside footing cord located across batter boards. Remove outside footing cords from batter boards, but leave batter boards in place. They are needed later.

Now make preparation for a concrete poured footing. In most cases forms are not required since the sides of the trench generally serve the purpose. Make the leveling pegs, one for every 10 feet of trench. Scrap pieces of wood, roughly 1 x 2s and long enough for showing depth of concrete footing, plus a length when driven into the ground, will remain solidly in place.

Begin in middle of trench at one of the corners. Drive in a leveling peg part way into the ground (shown by arrow) with a hammer, leaving enough wood exposed to show footing depth. In the example, the thickness is 8 inches. Now move down the trench about 10 feet, in the direction of your choice, driving in next peg partly in the ground so when leveling board A rests on top of the two pegs, the level B positioned on top edge of board indicates level. Repeat process around perimeter of trench, always locating a peg in a corner position. When you've made the round, the first and last peg should indicate level when checked with leveling board and level. If they don't, recheck peg elevations until proper correction is made.

I recommend using readi-mix concrete for pouring the footing. However, to do your own mixing, see Appendix, Table I, for proportions of cement, rock, sand, and water. In either case, pour complete footing in one operation. Using two pieces of 2 x 4 fastened together in a T, puddle concrete level in trench and flush with tops of pegs. If you plan to pour a foundation or a combination of foundation and wall on top of footing, sink beveled pieces of 2 x 4s between pegs and flush with their tops. When footing has hardened, remove 2 x 4s, thereby forming a key slot to give a good bond to the foundation. *Caution:* Use old crankcase oil to grease the 2 x 4s before setting

them into the concrete. This makes for easy removal once the concrete has hardened.

## CONSTRUCTING THE FOUNDATION AND WALLS

A *foundation* is constructed on the middle part of the footing. A *wall* might be thought of as an extension of the foundation to approximately 2 feet 6 inches above ground level. Sometimes the wall and foundation are made of masonry and constructed in one operation. Alternately a foundation may consist of concrete blocks or poured concrete with a wall of bricks, stone, wood (preferably redwood), and asbestos boards. In other cases, the framework is fastened onto a foundation consisting of poles set in the ground.

### Wood Pole Foundation

*IV-10*

**IV-10.** The layout of a wood pole foundation is generally the same as described previously, with the exception of the footing—none is required. Because a footing is not required, batter boards are not necessary.

Once building edge lines are fastened to nails in top of building corner stakes and on the same horizontal plane, locate and dig holes with a post hole digger to accommodate wood poles approximately 6 inches in diameter. Dig four corner holes inside the building edge lines. Then dig inbetween holes 6 feet on centers with exception of posts nearest corner posts. Here center of inbetween posts should be 6 feet from outside edge of corner posts as shown in the picture. Now set poles 6 inches in diameter and long enough so bottoms are below frost line. Use poles that are pressure-treated and nontoxic to plants. For a substantial foundation, poles should be 3 feet in length. Generally, greenhouse plans call for a built-up, pressure-treated sill assembly fastened onto the wood poles. *Caution:* Under no circumstances use a wood preservative toxic to plants in or around the greenhouse.

## Concrete Block Foundation

IV-11

**IV-11.** Other than a wheelbarrow or mixing box and some of the tools used in preparing the footing, tools required to construct a masonry foundation are shown in the picture. The glossary gives definition and/or use of each.

| | | | |
|---|---|---|---|
| 1. | Framing square | 5. | Line block |
| 2. | Garden hoe | 6. | Jointer tool, |
| 3. | Bricklayer's | | optional. |
| | trowel | | Picture shows a tool |
| 4. | Brick set | | used to rake joints. |

Begin by replacing building edge lines across batter boards and in the building-edge saw kerfs. Using plumb bob locate and mark corner points on footing. Using a chalk line, with the aid of a helper, connect the four corner points, forming the building edges around perimeter of footing.

To bond the concrete blocks you can use factory mixed mortar, available in sacks from a local lumberyard, or you can prepare mortar by mixing 1 part Portland cement to 4 parts of clean sand to 1 part of hydrated lime. First thoroughly mix the ingredients *dry* in a wheelbarrow or mortar box, using a hoe. Then, slowly add clean water as you mix them into a smooth plastic-like paste until it slips easily from the trowel without running. If sand contains particles larger than ¼ inch,

screen through a piece of ¼-inch hardware cloth before using.

IV-12

**IV-12.** Here are a few steps for learning quickly how to "throw" mortar like a pro. First of all, don't grab the trowel as you would normally pick up a wrench, for instance. Rather, have thumb pressed against ferrule as shown by arrow, as you hold trowel loosely but firmly. From this day on, always hold trowel in this manner when laying any kind of masonry. It may feel clumsy at first, but with a little practice, you'll understand why there's no more practical way to hold a trowel.

IV-13a

**IV-13.** Hold trowel correctly with mortar side up, point down, on edge of face shell A. As mortar begins to slip from trowel, turn it slowly as you also move down side of face shell. Continue forward and downward movement as you continue turning the trowel, depositing mortar all the time. Actually, your trowel should turn gradually from beginning to end of stroke when it completes a half circle and trowel is in a vertical or plumb position. Spread enough mortar for laying at least

IV-13b

IV-13c

a couple of blocks, then spread an equal amount of mortar on opposite face shells B. The illustrations show trowel without mortar, so its positions can be clearly seen as it moves down face shells.

of blocks.) Next draw point of trowel through mortar forming furrow. This step makes for a good bond by concentrating mortar along face shells. Now place corner block which has one flat end for forming corners, exactly where layout is indicated by building-edge marks on footing. Using trowel handle, tap block down level and plumb until height of block plus mortar bed equals 8 inches. Continue laying blocks on the footing, level and plumb until the corner is formed. Then check corner for squareness with a carpentry framing square. If you used a level, each block will be level and plumb and corner will be exactly square.

IV-14

IV-15

**IV-14.** Once the practice sessions are over you are ready to lay blocks. (Note: Actual dimensions of blocks are ⅜ inch short of their stated dimensions. Thus, an 8 x 8 x 16-inch block is really 7⅝ x 7⅝ x 15⅝ inches. The ⅜-inch difference is made up by the mortar joint. In short, the laying of one such block and one mortar joint gives a height of exactly 8 inches.) Check with building plan often so foundation complies exactly with stated dimensions.

Lay up corners first. Begin at any corner you wish. Predampen footing for laying initial course on a full bed of mortar. For a good bond, spread enough mortar from your trowel the wall width over footing. (Note: Some masons do not follow this practice. They simply throw mortar to fall directly under outside face shells of the first layer

**IV-15.** Next spread mortar from trowel for second course *only* along two outer face shells, leaving crosswebs bare. Because face shells are narrow, do *not* furrow mortar as in first course laid on footing. *Caution:* If you are subject to a building code, check it. Some codes call for a full bed of mortar bedding on each course of blocks. This means mortar on crosswebs as well as on face shells. Position corner block. Then level it by tapping it, closing mortar joint to ⅜ inch. Lay remaining corner blocks as shown in picture.

Mortar must be placed on each vertical joint, also. This is easily done by standing block on end. Mortar sticks best when it is slapped on and wiped across the corner. Next pick up block and shove it vertical and plumb against block previously placed. Continue until corner has two or three courses, whichever you prefer. Always shove and tap each block downward and toward adjoining block. As corner goes up, be sure to check each course with a rule. Tops of blocks should not only be level and plumb, they also should reach heights in multiples of 8 inches, such as 8, 16, 24 inches, etc. Do not tap or move block after mortar sets. To do so breaks the bond. Rather, remove block, clean off mortar, remortar and relay it.

Next build up two or three courses of blocks on remaining three corners. As you work, your mortar will have a tendency to become stiff. In this case, mix a little water with it so you won't have to pound too hard to close the joint to its ⅜-inch thickness. Never try to thin mortar that has begun to set. When this happens, throw it away and mix a new batch.

*IV-16*

**IV-16.** Use trowel as shown in picture for cutting off excess mortar, making flush joints. Use excess mortar for buttering end of block. Check end joints as you proceed, being sure they are completely filled with mortar.

Make flush joints in the foundation. If your plans call for a concrete block wall, you can continue making flush joints above the foundation, or you can tool them. I recommend using a concave jointing tool for making concave joints. *Caution:* When the flush joints are hard enough

to thumb print, smooth and compact them with a jointing tool. Tool vertical joints first, then tool horizontal joints.

*IV-17*

**IV-17.** Using two line blocks, stretch a nylon line between top edge of first course in two opposite corners. The cord is used as a guide to lay inbetween blocks to. A line block is a small, specially cut wooden or metal piece used to hold a line stretched between two opposite masonry corners to serve as a guideline for the mason to lay concrete blocks, bricks, or stones in a straight, horizontal line. Picture shows one kind of line block. Usually, you can obtain a couple of line blocks free from your cement supplier. Using techniques mentioned above, lay blocks by beginning at each corner and working toward center of first course. Be sure top edges almost touch the line. Corner blocks and inbetween blocks should all be laid in the same horizontal plane. Here the trick is to set line blocks so a space of about $\frac{1}{32}$ inch exists between line and corner blocks. By not touching line, wall does not "belly out" as a result of inbetween blocks shoving line into a slight curve.

Spread mortar on top of face shells for only three or four blocks ahead. The idea is to keep only enough fresh mortar ahead for laying as many blocks as you can without it becoming dry. In extremely hot, dry weather, I spread only enough mortar for laying one block at a time. (Note: If you use blocks above the foundation for a wall, be sure to use recessed jamb blocks on both sides of door opening. They come in full and half length sizes from your block source.)

If your walls are made of blocks, don't forget to string electric cables for wall outlets and switches through the cores of the blocks, then out through openings made with a hammer and cold chisel. Make opening by marking outline of box on block at desired opening location. Then score with chisel. Continue tapping score lines around box outline with chisel until piece breaks out. Then bring wires through holes in outlet box and mortar in place. Prepare mortar by using 2 parts Portland cement to 1 part clean sand mixed with clear water. Use the bricklayer's trowel to place mortar, cutting off excess between box and block. For further information on electric wiring, see Chapter VI.

*IV-19*

mer and brick set to score both sides of block. Then place block on flat, solid surface. Tilt set outward with bevel facing away from edge to be exposed (undercut). Then strike it a hard blow with the hammer. *Caution:* Always wear safety glasses when cutting any type of masonry. Also, do not allow others to stand near unless their eyes are protected.

Continue laying inbetween blocks until all four walls reach top course of corners. Then continue building up corners, followed by inbetween blocks, until desired height of foundation or wall is reached.

*IV-18*

**IV-18.** The last block, laid in the middle of a course, is called a closing block—you will probably have to cut a block to fit the final gap, see details below. Lay closing block by buttering joints with four ribbons of mortar on block and four on adjoining blocks making up course. (Note: Laying a closing block may try your patience, but practice and will power can give you a pro's touch.)

**IV-19.** A masonry saw cuts concrete blocks as easily as a power saw cuts wood, but it isn't really necessary to obtain one. You can do an acceptable job of cutting blocks with a brick set, purchasable at most hardware stores. Use a ham-

*IV-20*

**IV-20.** Complete the block laying job by concreting in ½ x 18-inch anchor bolts, placed about 6 feet apart along top two courses of foundation,

if a wall is not in your plans. If you lay a block wall, grout in the bolts on the last two courses of it instead. Begin by pushing squashed newspapers two courses down to form a temporary base for retaining the concrete. Make concrete by mixing 1 part Portland cement to 2 parts sand to 4 parts small rock to enough clean water to make a putty-like mixture. Position bolts, heads down, in center of holes with 2 inches extending above top course. Fill holes with concrete flush with top of blocks. When concrete has hardened (at least 72 hours) use a 2-inch wood sill bored to fit over anchor bolts. Then place washers on top of sill, following by nuts to draw it down against top course. The purpose of sill is to furnish a base firmly fastened to foundation or wall onto which the greenhouse is constructed. Use a sill that is treated with a wood preservative nontoxic to plants.

## Poured Concrete Foundations

Generally, poured concrete foundations fall into one or two classifications. There are low foundations, such as found in hotbeds, cold-frames, and greenhouses not having solid concrete poured walls. Then there are high foundations, which actually are a combination of wall and foundation. Generally, these do not exceed 30 inches in height.

For building either the low or high poured concrete foundation, the only tools required are a shovel, saw, hammer, and a scrap piece of 2 x 4 to smooth top.

Locate four corner stakes, spaced to meet your requirements as previously explained in this chapter on laying out the foundation.

**IV-21.** For supporting a hotbed or coldframe, dig a footing trench 4 inches wide to a depth of 6 inches below the frost zone around perimeter of bed, being sure outside of trench coincides with outside dimensions of proposed hotbed or cold-frame bed. Next flare bottom of trench 2 inches on each side to serve as a footing form. If your frost line is very deep, it is difficult to dig trench with a shovel. One way to maintain a 4-inch wall is to dig trench as wide as shovel width. Then in following step, build inside form from footing top to required foundation height. Loose dirt tamped in place as well as stakes can be used to hold inside form boards in line. If you prefer to use 4 x 8 x 16-inch concrete blocks on top of

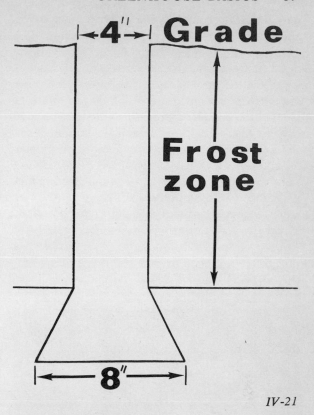

IV-21

footing instead of poured concrete, refer to previous section of this chapter on laying blocks.

IV-22

**IV-22.** Build the form with 2 x 4s fastened together at the corners with 16-penny box nails for inside and outside forms, inside faces forming continuous plane with excavation walls. Hold in place with 1 x 2-inch stakes placed between 2 and 3 feet apart as shown in the picture. Then tamp concrete inside trench and wood form. If you made a trench, be sure to fill flared portion of its bottom. Use a scrap piece of lumber or a trowel to strike off concrete on top of forms. (Note: Lightly tamping outside of form makes for a smooth concrete foundation.) If your concrete requirement is for a half cubic yard or more, have a company deliver readi-mix. For a smaller amount, it is usually cheaper to mix the concrete yourself, because most companies have an expensive minimum charge that makes small deliveries impractical. See Appendix, Table I, for mixing instructions. When concrete has set for 48 hours, remove forms, cleaning them immediately if you wish to reuse them. In the picture, the 2 by 4s rest on scrap lumber positioned between inside forms, this serves to hold them in place because they were sawed half in two to make inside form removal easier once the concrete hardened.

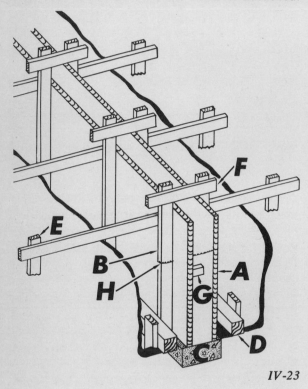

*IV-23*

**IV-23.** The illustration shows how to build forms for a combination foundation and wall supported on footings. For minimum marring and maximum strength, use two-headed or duplex nails to fasten ⅝ or ¾-inch plywood A to 2 x 4 form studs B spaced on 24-inch centers. Interior grade plywood can be reused a couple of times and is cheaper than exterior grade plywood. Use a minimum number of nails so forms are easy to take apart for reuse of lumber. Position forms on middle of footing C. Use 4 x 4s or two 2 x 4s as braces D staked in place to hold bottom of form in place. Hold top of form in vertical position with 2 x 4 stakes and braces E, and 1 x 4

ties F nailed in place. Use 2 16-penny box nails where 2 x 4s join and 2 8-penny box nails where 1 x 4 ties are fastened to 2 x 4 studs. To further aid in keeping walls from spreading apart, join studs on opposite sides with #10 tie rods H, which you can obtain from your concrete supplier. Place ties H every 2½ feet vertically. (Note: for a combination greenhouse foundation and wall 4 feet high, I place a tie in the middle of wall at each stud.) It is a good idea to place 1 x 2 spacers G at each tie location to keep walls properly spaced. Following removal of forms, break off snap ties. Break occurs 1 inch back of surface. Touch up noticeable holes above grade with mortar made by mixing 2 parts Portland cement and 1 part sand with enough clean water to produce a pliable mix. Protect form position by pouring the concrete slowly from ends to middle of form and preferably in layers 6-12 inches thick. Be sure to pour entire form in one operation. Use a short piece of 2 x 4 to strike off concrete level with top of form. *Caution:* If your plans call for sill bolts to be fastened in top of wall, install them immediately following strike off. (*Note:* Remove spacers G as concrete is being poured.)

Unless you can reuse walls and stud materials and form lumber, it might be cheaper for you to have the walls poured by a professional concrete finisher, who has reusable metal forms.

## FLOORS, WALKS, AND DRIVEWAYS

Unless the greenhouse is a part of the home, such as a solarium or sunroom, a solid floor is not recommended. Poured concrete walks, however, are most practical when built between the benches. Crushed rock, river gravel, or small pebbles used for groundcover under benches provide humidity and drain excess water. A poured concrete driveway is something else to consider during the planning stage, especially if you plan to make deliveries by truck from inside the greenhouse out through a garage-type door.

### Poured Concrete Walks

**IV-24.** In addition to a carpenter's hammer, nylon cord, level, garden rake, a fiber push broom, and a 2 x 4 strike off board (length about a foot wider than width of walk), masonry tools required for building poured concrete walks and

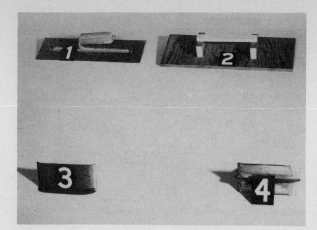

IV-24

place with 1 x 2-inch stakes driven into ground flush with cords. In the picture, excess dirt is lightly packed on outside of form to help hold sides straight. If form boards do not stay put, hold them firm by driving a 6-penny box nail through stake into 2 x 4. For dry walks, set top of forms slightly above grade with one side about ½ inch higher than the other. Use a level to check.

driveways are illustrated. Glossary gives definition and/or use of each.

1. Cement finisher's metal trowel
2. Wood or metal hand float
3. Edger
4. Double edger

Concrete, 2 x 4s for building forms, and 1 x 2-inch pointed stakes (which you can cut from scrap lumber), a few 6-penny box nails, and some polyethylene are the materials required.

IV-26

**IV-26.** If truck crossings are planned or if you want an exceptionally strong walk, place reinforcement wire mesh, such as 6 x 6-10/10, on top of subgrade inside forms. Wire fabric is usually available in rolls 5 or 6-feet wide. Most dealers offer fractional rolls for sale. The two pairs of numbers indicate the size and style of the fabric. The numbers are pronounced six, six, ten, ten. The first pair of numbers refers to wire spacing—6 inches apart each way. The second pair of numbers refers to the wire gauge longitudinal and transverse—10-gauge for both. The larger the gauge, the lighter the wire. If you want curved walks, use strips of plywood or hardboard, such as Masonite, 3½ inches wide as part of the form as shown in the picture. Place ½-inch asphalt expansion strips in the form to serve as expansion joints about 20 feet apart, cutting reinforcement wire mesh, if you use it, at each joint location. The 2 x 4s within the form are used as spreaders. They are removed just before the concrete reaches them.

IV-25

**IV-25.** First prepare the subgrade. Use a nylon cord stretched between two end stakes on each side of proposed walk to establish outside edges of 2 x 4 form. Then, with a shovel, scoop out about 3 inches of dirt (a 2 x 4 placed on edge is 3½ inches thick) between the cords. Remove all organic matter (sod, roots, etc.) and fill cavities that form with well-tamped dirt.

Reset cords to desired width and grade of walk. Then place top edge of straight 2 x 4 to approximately 1/16 inch from line. Hold form lumber in

**IV-27.** If you wish to mix your own concrete, see Appendix, Table I, however, I recommend using readi-mix concrete. When you place the order tell the clerk you are building walks and

IV-27

he will send concrete with the required ingredients properly mixed. Just before truck is expected, hose down the subgrade if it is dry or is of a sandy consistency. This smooths out rough spots and prevents the concrete from setting too quickly. Be sure no puddles of water remain. When the truck arrives, instruct the operator to pour slowly as you or a helper (working with concrete is a two-man job) use a garden rake to spread the concrete level between the form boards. As you spread, also use the rake to pull reinforcement wire mesh (if used) up into lower half of concrete layer.

IV-28

**IV-28.** As soon as the concrete is raked evenly between the forms, use a 2 x 4, approximately 1 foot wider than the form, to strike off the surface. Do not drag the 2 x 4 in a single operation. Rather, work it back and forth as you slowly move along outside the form, as indicated by arrows in the picture. This operation helps to push large ingredients (rock) downward and bring small ingredients (sand and cement) to the surface. This operation should not be overworked. Generally, one moves the 2 x 4 from one end of

form to the other end and back again before obtaining a smooth surface. Always keep a little concrete built up in front of the 2 by 4 during the smoothing operation. This is sometimes referred to as the strike-off operation.

IV-29

**IV-29.** The next operation is called floating; some concrete finishers say, "laying it down." This means further pushing the rock down and bringing the sand and cement to the surface. How long to wait between striking-off and floating depends upon the weather, which governs the amount of water remaining on top of the concrete. When the temperature is around 70°F., I find concrete ready for floating in about thirty minutes after the strike-off. Look for these signs: as the water begins to evaporate, the concrete takes on a light gray color. This makes for a dull surface. Try floating. If trowel digs in and concrete doesn't want to level out, wait until a grayer or duller appearance shows on the surface. One word of caution. You cannot wait too long before floating, or the concrete will begin to set. To be on the safe side, until you have more experience, make several trial runs right after the concrete surface begins to take on a grayish cast and appears duller than when first struck off. If you desire a smooth, gritty surface, this is the final operation of actual finishing. If this is what you want, move into the edging and double-edging operations described later.

**IV-30.** If you prefer a slick finish, use a steel, rectangular concrete finisher trowel in light, even, wide-arc strokes with blade held perfectly level on top of surface. Again look for more graying of surface before beginning troweling operation. If trowel digs into concrete, either concrete is not cured enough or trowel is being used in a slight

*IV-30*

*IV-32*

angle rather than parallel to the surface. Generally, going over surface two or three times produces a slick surface, leveling any trowel marks that might have been made inadvertently. If concrete sets too rapidly, sprinkle water lightly on surface with a paint brush. (Note: If water must be used, sprinkle sparingly as if you were stranded in a desert and had only a cup of water between you and dehydration. Too much water at this point washes away cement, leaving the sand. When the excess water dries, small shallows remain. This means puddles on the walk during wet weather.)

*IV-31*

**IV-31.** Use an edging tool, curve of tool next to form, to give outside surface a professional look. Actually, edging and grooving (described in the following step) go hand in hand with finishing with the steel trowel. If you do *all* the troweling first, you may find it almost impossible to force the edger and double edger down properly in the concrete. Generally, the pros alternate between trowel, edger, and double edger, ensuring that they force rock down near edge and joints before the final use of the three tools.

**IV-32.** Use a double edger (sometimes called a groover) next to a 2 x 4 for making joints at right angles to the form. There is no firm and fast rule on spacing these joints. It is common practice, however, for the joints and expansion strips to make up a uniform pattern. For a walk 2 feet wide, I make joints 3 feet apart. While joints add an attractive look to the walk, they serve a practical purpose. In most climates the walk will eventually develop cracks. Deep joints and expansion joints provide weakened areas which are natural places for cracks to occur. This leaves little chance for unsightly zigzag cracks to form across the walk. Marks will form on one side of edger and on both sides of double edger. Use steel trowel to remove them. If you do not care for a slick finish, use the steel trowel only long enough to produce a relatively smooth surface, then use a fiber broom lightly over the surface to form a straight line pattern. One can also form a nonslip surface with a fiber broom by making a swirl pattern. When concrete has stiffened to the point of supporting your weight without marring the surface, spread plastic sheeting over it to help retard evaporation. Then prevent concrete from curing too fast by spraying it with water periodically for four to six days. Then remove plastic sheeting. About four weeks are required for concrete to reach its maximum strength. You can, however, walk on it right after the plastic sheeting is removed.

**Driveways**

Essentially, poured concrete driveways are built in the same way described in Fig. IV-26 for poured concrete walks; there are these differences:

Reinforce with 6 x 6-6/6 wire fabric. As you

spread concrete with a rake, also pull wire fabric upward so that it is approximately 2 inches from bottom of slab. Another way to position wire fabric is to place it on the subgrade with enough 2-inch rocks underneath to hold it in position during the concrete pouring operation. Place ½-inch expansion joints about 30 feet apart. Make either a broom-swept or a wood-float finish as a slick steel-trowel finish is not desirable for driveways.

## WINDBREAKS

If your greenhouse location does not afford protection from prevailing winds, add a windbreak of trees or a wood fence. You will need a post hole digger to install a wooden fence.

**IV-33.** The picture shows an ideal spot for building a greenhouse. Junipers, planted in a straight row, afford ample protection during the cold blasts of winter as well as during early spring and late fall. If the trees are kept trimmed to prevent solid foliage developing, wind speeds will be slowed. A spraying with Isotox, diluted with water as described on the label, when bag worms are born in late spring (in my area June 1 is the time I set aside to do the job) keeps these plants relatively free of insects. (Note: Isotox is available at most nurseries and hardware stores.)

Purchasing trees tall enough to protect the greenhouse can cut deeply into the greenhouse budget. One way to lick that problem is to plant small trees and at the same time build a cheap fence parallel to them. When the trees have grown, remove the fence. Some greenhouse owners build a permanent windbreak fence at the outset.

**IV-34.** A board-on-board fence is easy to build and affords privacy as well as providing a suitable windbreak. Stretch a nylon cord between two wood stakes driven into the ground to mark

*IV-33*

fence location. Next place stakes 8 feet apart on centers to indicate post locations. Dig post holes about 8 inches in diameter and half as deep as posts extend above the ground. In this case, depth is 4 feet. Place 12-foot x 4 x 4-inch treated posts A or redwood posts, which are not subject to decay, loosely in holes. Then backfill end posts either with tamped earth, gravel, or concrete (in that order, depending on whether you desire a short, medium, or long post life). As you do so, use a carpenter's level to ensure posts set perpendicular. Next stretch a cord between bottoms of end posts and a cord between the tops. Now set inbetween posts, using the top and bottom cords as guidelines; be certain tops of posts lie in the same horizontal plane. Fasten 2 x 4-inch stringers B on top of posts with 16-penny box nails. If your posts were set on 8-foot centers, joints will always fall on one of the posts, providing you purchased lumber in multiples of 8 feet. Use 16-penny box nails to toenail (see glossary) two sets of 2 x 4 stringers C in between posts. Fasten one set about 8 inches above grade, the other midway between bottom set and top stringers B. Using either treated or galvanized 8-penny box nails, fasten 1 x 6-inch boards D, spaced 5 inches apart (a 1 x 6 board is 5½ inches wide) on both sides of stringers as shown. (Note: Use a 1 x 10-

*IV-34*

inch board to start and finish the fence.) Such spacing reduces speed of air moving through fence. Alternating boards on either side of stringers gives the board-on-board effect for which fence is named.

Complete job by painting fence two coats of exterior paint. If you use treated posts, wait about three months before painting them. Immediate painting makes the treatment bleed through the paint.

# V

# Plumbing

If you are subject to a building code, check plumbing requirements before making installations. Poorly designed plumbing can disrupt the most efficient gardening program. The recommendations on installations in this chapter have all withstood the test of time! Install hot and cold water lines to the workbench, lead drain to sanitary sewer or septic tank. Use adequately sized pipes but make main lines and branch lines as short as possible. Insulating hot water lines does much to conserve on energy and save on heating bills. Be sure to install water pipes below frost line. If you have hot water lines running under ground, wrap them in an asbestos-type insulation, then lay them inside 4-inch plastic pipe. Bring this pipe at least 6 inches above grade inside the greenhouse. Be certain to use proper solvent, described later in this chapter, to seal pipes into fitting sockets. If water supply pipes or drain pipes are to pass under driveway, lay them deep enough in the ground to avoid damage by heavy traffic.

Locate several garden hose valves within the greenhouse, then several shorter pieces of hose can be used. This is preferable to installing a single valve with one cumbersome hose of 50 feet. Place valves high enough so you do not have to stoop when using them. If containers are to be placed under them, leave plenty of room.

Probably, the luxury of a bath near the greenhouse is not necessary, but a toilet bowl and a sink installed in a building adjoining or near the greenhouse will keep you in the good graces of the lady of the house. She will be most appreciative for your having done so during wet weather when you and the hired help fail to leave muddy footprints from the back door to the bathroom. Other than fixtures, the greenhouse plumbing system consists of two areas: 1. an adequate water supply system; and 2. a safe drainage system. Plastic pipes are recommended and illustrated because they are lightweight, require only a few common tools to install, and are simple enough for anyone. They have some fittings designed for water supply and some for drainage, each excellent for its intended job.

Even if the mention of plumbing mystifies you, forget such inhibitions! You really can install your own system for the greenhouse. The few instructions on selecting and connecting pipes and fittings are simple and given in logical, sequential order, with illustrations.

**V-1.** The illustration literally removes the water supply pipes and the drainage system parts from their hiding places between walls, under floors, and in the ground. Study this picture carefully, first as you estimate the plumbing requirements, then as you make the installations.

## SUPPLY SYSTEM PARTS

1. Stop and waste valves. Install at low point of cold and hot water lines as they enter the greenhouse.

2. Cold water main line. It serves two or more fixtures or pieces of equipment requiring cold water.

3. Hot water main line. It serves two or

46

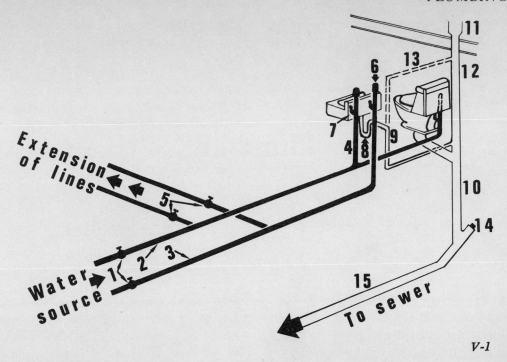

*V-1*

more fixtures, if required, in the greenhouse.

4. Branch line to fixture. A line (hot or cold) designed to serve one fixture only.

5. Shutoff valves. One required in each branch line, and in all main lines if cutoff is required.

6. Anti-hammer. Optional, unless you like to hear water pipes banging. To prevent pipe banging, install one in each branch line where it is connected to a faucet.

7. Fixture supply line. A section of a branch line leading directly to one fixture only.

## SEWAGE AND DRAINAGE SYSTEM PARTS

8. Fixture drain. A section of branch drain leading away from a specific fixture. For health reasons, each requires a trap (as shown in the picture) or has trap built-in. The purpose of traps is to prevent gases escaping into the greenhouse.

9. Branch drain. A drain line leading away from one fixture only.

10. Soil stack. Vertical pipe, generally three or four inches in diameter, into which branch drains empty.

11. Vent increaser. Uppermost length of stack. It is larger in diameter than the stack proper and is required by some building codes, especially in extremely cold climates.

12. Vent. Top end of soil stack. It is from this end that gases escape into the air.

13. Re-vent. A bypass for air and gases between a branch drain and the vent part of the stack. This prevents fast flowing liquids leaving fixtures from sucking *all* of the liquid from the trap, which would allow gases to escape into the greenhouse.

14. Cleanout. Install one at points where obstruction may appear. A good rule of thumb is to install a tee with a pipe plug in one opening instead of an elbow in all drain lines. By all means install one at the foot of the stack as shown in the picture.

15. Greenhouse drain. Be sure all wastes drain toward stack, thence through main drain to final destination, such as a sump or a sanitary sewer.

(Note: Be sure dealer supplies you with rough measurements for all fixtures and pieces of equipment requiring water.)

### Water Supply System

In laying out both the hot and cold water lines, use no smaller plastic pipe than ¾-inch I.D. for main lines and ½-inch I.D. for branch lines. Install a shutoff valve near source of water supply.

This may be a continuation of your home water supply system or a special supply system located inside the greenhouse. Also, pitch the pipes slightly so they drain toward shutoff valve. This valve provides a means of draining the system for repairs; and a drainable system prevents costly repairs in a cold climate if the greenhouse is closed during the winter. To avoid hammering noises when faucets are closed, install anti-hammers in hot and cold lines prior to their attachment to fixture.

V-2

**V-2.** The only tools required for installing plastic water supply and drain pipes are 1, hacksaw, and 2, wrench, used to tighten adapters to threaded metal fittings. See glossary for use and/or definition.

V-3

**V-3.** Use plastic water supply pipes designed for the job you have in mind. Some plastic pipe is designed to carry only cold water. Other plastic pipe is designed only for indoor use. I recommend Chlorinated polyvinyl chloride (CPVC) water pipe because it is designed for indoor and outdoor use with hot and cold water. Be sure to use the solvent specifically recommended for the type of plastic pipe purchased. The pictrue shows fittings used in making the connections.

1. Tee
2. 90° elbow
3. 45° elbow
4. Coupling
5. Cap
6. Reducer bushing
7. Malye I.P. adapter
8. Strap

Begin by making a layout of your particular needs. Plan to use reducer bushings to connect larger pipes to smaller ones, such as a ¾-inch main line to a ½-inch branch line. Connect pipes of the same diameter with couplings. If you expect to extend the water line in the future, fasten a nipple (2- to 6-inch piece of water pipe) with a pipe cap cemented on one end and opposite end cemented to a coupling, which in turn is cemented to end of water pipe. Use 1-inch roofing nails for mounting pipes with straps.

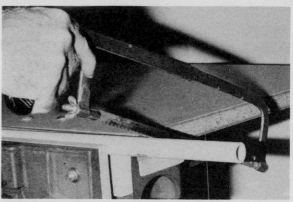

V-4

**V-4.** Use a hacksaw, or a tube cutter if you have one, to cut ends of pipe square.

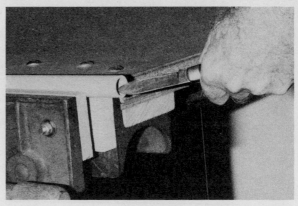

V-5

**V-5.** Using a pocketknife, carefully ream inside of pipe. *Caution:* Never leave fragments in pipe, the obstruction prevents faucets and valves from closing.

**V-6.** Use a nonsynthetic brush to apply solvent (designed for your kind of pipe) to inside of fitting socket and to outside surface of pipe to a distance equal to depth of socket.

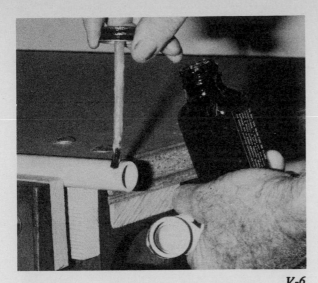

V-6

**V-7.** Give fitting ¼ turn as you push it over pipe. Fitting must be properly bottomed and aligned before solvent begins to set. Let assembly remain put until joint sets, otherwise fitting and pipe may pull apart. Follow setting time instructions on can of solvent. If excess solvent oozes around outside of fitting or pipe, wipe off before laying assembly down to set. Work on other pipes and fittings while waiting for previous ones to set.

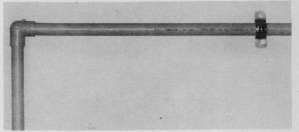

V-8

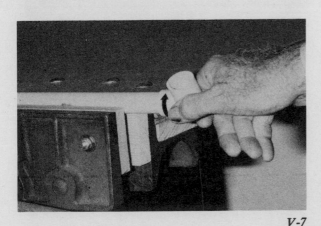

V-7

**V-8.** Using either plastic or metal straps and 1-inch roofing nails, support both vertical and horizontal runs at 3-foot intervals, being sure straps are not located closer than 3 feet to a 45° or a 90° turn. This arrangement allows normal contraction and expansion to take place without damaging cemented joints. *Caution:* When installing straps be sure pipe can pass through them freely, this provides free movement during contraction and expansion.

**V-9.** Attach faucets to workbench sink. Next connect faucets to cold and hot water lines. Screw male adapter into shutoff valve before cementing plastic supply pipe to socket. Generally, tightening with a wrench one turn past hand-tight is tight enough. The first illustration here shows a floor-type installation, while the second illustration shows a wall-type installation.

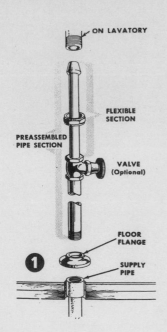

V-9a

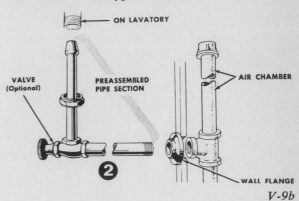

V-9b

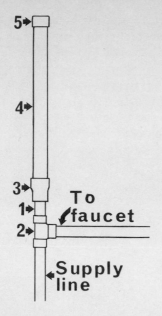

*V-10*

## Safe Drainage Systems

A greenhouse drainage system must provide complete and final disposal of waste water. Ask your supplier for plastic pipe especially designed for drainage use. I recommend rubber styrene (RS) plastic sewer and drainage pipe because it is designed for use indoor or underground. Pipes for drainage systems are not the same as those used for water supply lines, and neither one should ever be substituted for the other. Drainage pipes are larger because the flow is entirely by gravity. Therefore, they should be pitched ¼ inch per foot toward point of disposal. Water supply pipes, on the other hand, are smaller because their flow is under pressure. The purpose of their slope is to allow gravity to come into play when the water is shut off and the lines are drained for repairs.

The drainage system consists of three parts. All are required, even if the only fixture is a sink at the workbench. The three parts are: (1) drainage lines; (2) traps; and (3) vent lines.

*Drainage lines* may be vertical or almost horizontal for the purpose of carrying waste water to the sanitary sewer or septic tank.

*Traps* may be separate parts or they may be a part of the fixture itself. They should be located close to the fixture and should be accessible.

**V-10.** Although some greenhouse installations do not include anti-hammers in water supply lines, I recommend their installation to prevent hammering noises when faucets are closed. Cement one end of short nipple 1 into tee 2, and other end of nipple into small end of reducer 3. Then cement a piece of 12-inch long pipe 4, one size larger than water supply pipe, into large end of reducer. Complete anti-hammer by capping 12-inch pipe with a pipe cap 5. Be sure to cement all joints well. Arrows show direction of water supply.

Use a female adapter to connect to metal garden hose valves and shutoff valve.

If you connect to a hot water tank, use a temperature relief valve set no higher than 212° F. Install valve into a galvanized tee so probe enters water in top of heater. Extend cold water supply and hot water discharge line in galvanized pipe a minimum of 12 inches from hot water heater. Connect plastic pipes to galvanized pipes with galvanized unions. Screw male adapter into union and tighten approximately one turn beyond hand-tight. Connect plastic pipe to male adapter, as previously described, to complete installation. For tight joints—and ones that are easily loosened if repairs are needed—always place pipe thread compound on threads of galvanized pipe before attaching galvanized fittings. (Note: Short pieces of threaded galvanized pipe and fittings as well as pipe thread compound, can be secured from most hardware stores.)

**V-11.** The first illustration here shows a floor-type installation; the second illustration shows a wall-type installation. Connect a male adapter to trap. Then cement drain line into adapter socket. Tighten all parts together, as pictured in the illustration.

VENT LINES, which extend upward through the roof, allow air to flow into or out of the drainage pipes, thus eliminating a partial vacuum by equalizing air pressure in the drainage system. This prevents the water from being sucked out of the traps, which would allow sewer gas to enter the building and become a health hazard by polluting the air.

**V-12.** In addition to tools used previously in making the hot and cold water installation, you will need a hand saw and shovel for making the drainage installation. You might need a jig, if you have difficulty sawing the 4-inch plastic soil pipe square (main line to sewer). Here two boards are nailed to a 2 by 4 as shown. Next, a line is marked

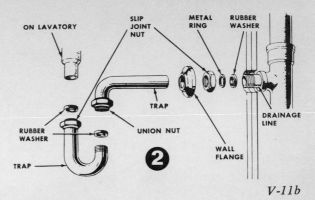

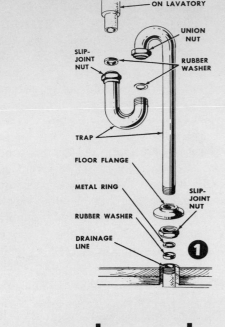

*V-11a*

*V-11b*

*V-12*

*V-13*

| | |
|---|---|
| 1. Solid pipe | 6. Reducer |
| 2. Coupling | 7. ¼ bend |
| 3. ⅛ bend | 8. Y |
| 4. ⅛ street bend | 9. Tee |
| 5. Hub end adapter | |

Here are guidelines for the drainage installation:

1. Pitch or slope pipes ¼ inch per foot for a desirable gravity flow on its way to final disposal into the sanitary sewer or septic tank line.

2. Never slope drainpipes more than suggested above. To do so can cause solids, such as paper, to clog the line. This happens when the water rushes away, leaving solids behind. The only exception is a 45° or 90° drop. In these cases, the pitch is great enough to carry both solids and waste water along their way at the same speed.

3. Exercise care in cementing joints totally so gases cannot leak.

4. Each fixture must have a vented trap to hold water. The trap acts as a seal, preventing sewer gases from passing into the greenhouse.

square on both sides. Then a hand saw is used to cut out the marks from top edge of boards to the 2 by 4. This makes sawing 1½-inch branch vent pipes, 3-inch drain pipes, and soil pipes square a simple operation when placed in the jig. To attach fittings to pipe be sure to use solvent specifically designed for the drain and vent pipes you are installing.

**V-13.** The picture shows pipe and fittings required for installing a safe greenhouse drainage system. The glossary gives definitions and/or uses. To prepare the pipe and use solvent on the fittings and pipe, follow the instructions previously given for water pipes and fittings.

# VI

# Electrical Installations

If you are not familiar with local and state electrical codes, check before making the installations to see how much of it, if any, you are permitted to handle. Sometimes, local or state code requirements supercede those of the National Electric Code. For instance, in this chapter nonmetallic cable, which meets the National Electric Code, is illustrated. For communities not accepting use of nonmetallic cable, thin-wall conduit is suggested. Also, check with your local power company and your fire-insurance agent. Usually, the only requirement is for the completed installation to be approved by a licensed electrician. Certain regulations may seem odd to you, but they are to safeguard you and other people working in the greenhouse, where damp conditions could make faulty electrical work particularly dangerous.

## GUIDELINES FOR SAFETY AND CONVENIENCE

1. Much mechanized equipment, including some electrical heating cable, operates on 230-volt power. If you plan to use such equipment, include a 230-volt as well as the more common 115-volt supply.

2. If you are installing a service panel in the greenhouse, use one requiring reset-type circuit breakers instead of that requiring replaceable fuses.

3. Plan the lighting circuits separate from those used for motors and heaters.

4. Install enough double service outlets to meet your needs. For convenience, locate them near top of greenhouse wall. If your greenhouse does not have walls, locate outlets on a solid surface 30–45 inches above the floor.

5. Place switches in convenient locations to control lights and other equipment. Make sure that motor switches are close to motor locations. Use two- and three-way switches, if they add to your convenience.

6. *All* switches and service outlets should be away from wet areas. For example, a service outlet too near a garden hose valve may be splashed with water. If an outlet must be located in such an area, use an outdoor, weatherproof receptacle.

7. Ground all metal objects. This includes switch, outlet, and light boxes (if metal), fans, heaters, and etc.

8. If you are going to talk either with people working outside the greenhouse or family inside your home, install an intercom system. It saves valuable time otherwise spent walking from place to place.

9. If you are a music lover, take advantage of having music broadcast over a loudspeaker to reduce monotony. Music played softly, so as not to interfere with normal speech, for short periods each hour helps to make greenhouse work more interesting and pleasing. Check the yellow pages for companies transmitting music as a commercial service to industrial and business places.

52

10. In recent years, as most greenhouse owners will attest, much has been accomplished in the field of using artificial light for growing better, larger, more beautiful plants. Furthermore, a few strips of proper fluorescent lights, well placed, can have a definite effect on plant growth. I recommend Number 775 Gro-lux fluorescent lamp, sold by National Greenhouse Company. This is Sylvania's new energy source for plants. It maintains optimum light quality and intensity for best plant growth, regardless of season. Research indicates a fluorescent lamp with this energy distribution produces high rates of photosynthetic activity in plants. This lamp makes it possible to use normally wasted greenhouse space. It uses any standard fluorescent ballast circuit, and consumes the same amount of electricity as standard fluorescent lamps of the same wattage rating. Use regular reflectors or channel fixtures from your local electrical supply house.

## WIRING, FIXTURES, AND EQUIPMENT INSTALLATION

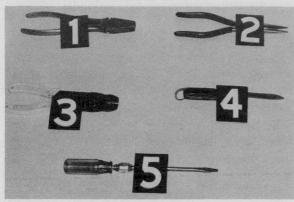

VI-1

**VI-1.** You will need a hacksaw and shovel used previously as well as the following tools for making the electrical installations. See glossary for definition and/or use of each.

1. Regular pliers
2. Long-nose pliers
3. Multipurpose wiring tool
4. Pocketknife
5. Screwdriver

The following list serves as a guide to materials required for greenhouse electrical installations:

### Electrical Installation Materials

| Name | Description |
|---|---|
| **OPTIONAL 115/230-VOLT SERVICE INSTALLATION** | |
| Service panel or branch service panel | Amperage to satisfy total amperage of greenhouse circuits, such as 100-, 150-, 200-ampere capacity. |
| Service wire | To run between meter box and service panel, size approved by utility company. |
| Service wire conduit and fittings | To cover and hold service wire in place between meter box and service panel, sizes as approved by the utility company. |
| Ground rod | Copper rod placed in the earth to serve as the ground for the electrical system, size as approved by the utility company. |
| Ground wire | To run between meter box and ground rod, size as approved by the utility company. |
| Ground wire conduit and fittings | To cover and hold ground wire in place between meter box and ground rod, sizes as approved by the utility company. |
| Ground wire clamp | Used to connect ground wire to ground rod. |
| **115-VOLT INSTALLATION** | |
| Rectangular metal boxes | Switch and service outlet boxes. Purchase type designed for kind of wiring used, such as nonmetallic, sheathed cable (kind shown in this chapter). |
| Octagonal metal boxes | Lighting and junction boxes. Purchase type designed for kind of wiring used, such as nonmetallic, sheathed cable or conduit. |
| Metal hangers | Fastened between 2 by material for the purpose of supporting metal boxes. Sometimes two 16-penny nails are used through holes in metal boxes to fasten them to structural wood members of the greenhouse framework. |
| Nails | 2-inch roofing nails, used for fastening box hangers to structural wood members. |

*(Table Continued)*

**Electrical Installation Materials—cont.**

| Name | Description |
|------|-------------|
| Wire | Three-wire (two wires plus bare ground wire) nonmetallic, sheathed cable unless conduit is required by local code. Size determined by your electrical plan. |
| Plastic cable | Covered, nonmetallic cable designed to run underground, code permitting. If not permitted, use the cable run through conduit. |
| Staples | Designed and used for holding nonmetallic cable in place on wood framing members. If conduit is used, fasten in place with straps designed for it. |
| Weatherproof receptacles | Designed for mounting outdoors. Should be used also inside greenhouse if water might splash on receptacle. |
| Switches | Single-pole, 3- or 4-way types, number, kind, and color (brown or yellow) in accordance with lighting plan. |
| Switch plates | Fastened to switch boxes. Number and color in accordance with lighting plan. |
| Service outlets | Number and color in accordance with lighting plan. |
| Service outlet plates | Fastened to outlet boxes. Number and color in accordance with lighting plan. |
| Electrician's plastic tape | Used as insulation to cover splices, taps, and wire connections if nonsolderless connectors are not used. |

230-VOLT INSTALLATION

| Name | Description |
|------|-------------|
| Service outlets and outlet boxes | Designed for 230-volt nonmetallic cable unless conduit is required. Outlet boxes are the same kind as those used for 115-volt outlets. Sometimes, however, two boxes joined together are required to accommodate a single outlet. |
| Three-wire cable | Nonmetallic, sheathed cable with each wire insulated or conduit sizes as called for in your electrical plan. (Note: Do not confuse this cable with three-wire nonmetallic cable designed to carry 115-volt current.) |

OPTIONAL INSTALLATIONS

| Name | Description |
|------|-------------|
| Electric soil-heating cable | Comes for either 115- or 230-volt circuits. |
| Electric motors | To run ventilating, cooling, and heating systems. |
| Thermostat | Used to control temperature automatically. |
| Humidistat | Used to control humidity automatically. |
| Temperature alarm with bell | Used to call attention when high or low temperature is reached. |
| Soil shredder | Labor-saving device used by florists, nurserymen, and vegetable growers to shred soil. |

## Installation Of Service Panel And Accessories

A separate electric meter and service panel for the greenhouse is optional. If your home service panel does not contain enough unused circuits to supply the electrical requirements for the greenhouse, you can install a branch service panel in the greenhouse; connect it to the take-off lugs on the main switch in your home service panel. Make the connection with the correct size plastic cable designed for underground use. If you do supply the greenhouse with electricity in this manner, the cable must be inside plastic pipe buried at least three feet under ground and to a point at least six inches above ground level where it enters and comes out of the ground. (See Chapter V for plastic pipe installation.) *Caution:* Before making installation, check local electric code. If weatherproof plastic cable encased in plastic pipe is not permitted underground, run the cable through conduit, making bends with a conduit bender, which you can rent. Also, see copper wire size tables, presented later in this chapter.

In order to carry the additional amperage, your original service wires from the electric line to the meter, and from the meter to the service panel, as well as the ground wire, must be sized large enough to deliver the total wattage required for both your home and the greenhouse. This is not the problem it appears. Your local power company will be glad to examine your present wiring system and advise you whether it will be cheaper to rewire between your home service panel and the electric line or to install a separate meter and service panel in the greenhouse.

If you elect to have the power company bring service wires to the greenhouse, be sure to request an underground installation from the electric line to the meter box. The small additional cost difference between underground installation and overhead installation of service wires is well worth the price. Not only does an underground installation mean that the natural look of your property will be unspoiled, but high winds or ice storms can never damage the service wires. Also, birds don't have a roosting place.

*VI-2*

**VI-2.** If you elect to install a separate meter and service panel for the greenhouse, first check with your local power company for their recommendation of the best meter location. At this time find out how much of the outside wiring, including conduit and fittings, is your responsibility, and whether you or the power company furnish the meter box. Also, obtain their recommendation on the best size of service panel, 100, 150, or 200 amperes, to meet your electrical requirements.

Use round-head screws to fasten service panel approximately five feet above the floor to a solid support, such as a post or framing member. Arrow

points to breakers connecting service panel circuits to service wires, which later permit disconnecting power from meter to service panel if repairs or additions are required. X indicates a 230-volt circuit breaker mounted in panel ready for connecting circuit wires.

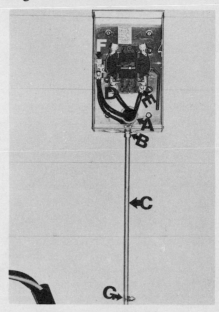

*VI-3*

**VI-3.** After removing knockout from rear of meter box, fasten conduit connector A in place for carrying service wires. Next remove knockout in bottom of box for ground wire conduit connector B. The power company will remove large knockout in bottom of box when installing service wires to the meter box, part of which are seen in the lower left corner of the picture.

Generally, power companies require mounting of meter box about five feet above grade. Cut hole through greenhouse wall for conduit connector A to fit snug. If you do not have a solid wall, such as the wall of a potting shed, office, etc., mount meter box on a solid supporting member of the greenhouse framework or mount it to a post adjacent to the framework. Be sure power company approves prior to installation.

Using ¼-inch round-head screws or bolts passing through mounting holes in meter box, fasten it securely in place. Trim about ½ inch of insulation from the three service wires to run from meter to service panel. Then remove clamps from the three lay-in terminals of meter box. Position two conductors (hot wires) into load terminals D and E and ground conductor (ground wire) into terminal F as shown. Replace clamps and tighten terminals D and E to 21 foot-pounds. (Note:

Tighten ground clamps later when ground wire to ground rod is attached.)

Next connect one end of service wire conduit to conduit connector A in rear of box and connect opposite end to a conduit connector installed in top of service panel, following removal of knock-out. If conduit run is long, do the following step along with conduit assembly. Wires are easier to string this way. (See Wiring With Thin-Wall Conduit, near end of this chapter.) Now work the three service wires through conduit connector A, then through conduit, until they come through conduit connector in top of service panel.

To complete your part of outside installation, work is continued outside. Next jog ground rod into the earth directly below conduit connector B located in bottom of meter box. Do this by using a shovel to dig a shallow hole about eight inches deep. Then fill with water. Holding ground rod with both hands, gently push it into the mud. Then raise it, allowing water to seep into hole. Repeat this operation over and over. Soon you will be surprised how easy it is to sink an 8-foot ground rod completely into the ground. Once you are under way, it is not necessary to bring bottom end completely out of the ground as you lift the rod. Raise it only far enough to allow water to fill the hole. *Caution:* Easy does it! Do not try to drive rod into the ground with a hammer or sledge. You could end up with the rod half out and half in and no way possible to remove it—short of mechanical power.

When top of ground rod is below surface to a depth recommended by the power company, cut a piece of conduit C to fit between it and conduit connector B. Use a hacksaw for cutting conduit to length. Then fasten one end of conduit C to conduit connector B; using conduit straps G every four feet, fasten conduit to wall. In most cases only one conduit strap is required.

Fasten and tighten with 21 foot-pounds of pressure one end of ground wire—ground wire does not require insulation—to solidly grounded neutral connection F in meter box.

**VI-4.** Now run ground wire through conduit connector in bottom of box on through conduit and out to ground rod. Using a special ground-rod clamp, fasten ground wire securely to ground rod as shown in the picture. The black plastic pipe to the left of the ground rod and ground rod clamp contain three service wires brought in by the power company.

*VI-4*

If you have not yet divided the lighting, service outlets, and motor equipment requirements into branch circuits, do so now. The number of branch circuits required depends upon the total number of watts possible from your electrical system. It is considered good practice to place lights, service outlets, and motor equipment on separate circuits. To do this, total anticipated wattage of the lights, then for service outlets, as well as for the motors—if your plans call for them. *Caution:* Use number of amperes required in starting a motor rather than number of amperes required once the motor is underway. If you find electrical equipment indicates amperes but not watts, find the wattage by multiplying voltage times amperes. Unless you plan to use equipment such as an air conditioner, that requires more than 2300 watts, I recommend limiting greenhouse branch circuits to 20 amperes each. The following table shows the relationship of maximum watts permitted in a branch circuit to copper wire size and size of circuit breaker:

**115-Volt Branch Circuit Requirements***

| Maximum watts | Copper Wire size | Circuit breaker in amperes |
|---|---|---|
| 1625 | 14 | 15 |
| 2300 | 12 | 20 |
| 3450 | 10 | 30 |
| 4600 | 8 | 40 |
| 6900 | 6 | 60 |

* Double maximum watts for same wire size and circuit breaker to figure 230-volt branch circuit requirements.

The copper wire sizes given in the table above are based on the assumption that length of wires are kept within required limits, allowing for a maximum voltage drop of 2 percent or less.

While installing main or branch circuits, make sure the wire sizes as given in the table above are not undersize for the distance they are to carry electricity. Undersize wires should not be used for two good reasons: 1. More than normal heat is created, resulting in wasted power; 2. More than normal voltage drop (a drop of 2 percent is considered acceptable) takes place, so that less than the required electrical capacity reaches the equipment. For, example, a cable containing two #12 wires plus ground will carry electricity a distance of 35 feet (one way) with only a 2 percent voltage drop. Run that same cable 90 feet (one way), and the voltage drops 5 percent. Rather than delve into electrical technicalities, the following tables are given for selecting cables with proper size wires for the distances they are to carry electricity:

#### Copper Wire Sizes (one-way distance) for Carrying 115 Volts

| Am-peres | Watts | No. 14 | No. 12 | No. 10 | No. 8 | No. 6 | No. 4 | No. 2 |
|---|---|---|---|---|---|---|---|---|
| 10 | 1,150 | 45' | 70' | 110' | 180' | 280' | 450' | 700' |
| 15 | 1,725 | 30' | 45' | 70' | 120' | 180' | 300' | 475' |
| 20 | 2,300 | 22' | 35' | 55' | 90' | 140' | 225' | 350' |
| 25 | 2,375 | 18' | 28' | 45' | 70' | 110' | 180' | 280' |
| 30 | 3,450 | 15' | 25' | 35' | 60' | 90' | 150' | 235' |

#### Copper Wire Sizes (one-way distance) for Carrying 230 Volts

| Am-peres | Watts | No. 14 | No. 12 | No. 10 | No. 8 | No. 6 | No. 4 | No. 2 |
|---|---|---|---|---|---|---|---|---|
| 10 | 2,300 | 90' | 140' | 220' | 360' | 560' | 900' | 1400' |
| 15 | 3,450 | 60' | 90' | 140' | 240' | 360' | 600' | 950' |
| 20 | 4,600 | 45' | 70' | 110' | 180' | 280' | 450' | 700' |
| 25 | 5,750 | 35' | 55' | 90' | 140' | 220' | 360' | 560' |
| 30 | 6,900 | 30' | 50' | 70' | 120' | 180' | 300' | 470' |

### Aluminum Wire

Although the Code approves the use of aluminum wire for greenhouse wiring, I recommend its use sparingly, certainly not for wiring the circuits.

Aluminum is a poor conductor of electricity, compared to copper. Therefore, it requires a larger wire to deliver the same voltage. Generally, electricians, if they use it, select an aluminum wire two sizes larger than copper wire. Although receptacles and switches with screw terminals, where the wire is wrapped around the screw, are suitable for making good connections, never fasten aluminum wire to friction-type or push-in terminals. Since aluminum oxidizes readily, soldered connections should be left to the expert.

Aluminum wire has one point in its favor: when a large electric cable is required for a long distance, it is considerably cheaper to use one containing aluminum wires two sizes larger than that required for copper wires. Take the example of the gardener who wanted to install a stand-by generator to supply electric power to home and greenhouse during brownouts. A cable of three #8 copper wires would cost $124.86. For $32.25 he bought a cable with three #4 aluminum wires; this delivered the same voltage as the copper wire cable.

### Installation Of Service Outlets, Lights And Switches In 115-Volt Circuit

Here are instructions on connecting service outlets, lights, and switches with nonmetallic cable. Be sure operations do not violate local or state codes. Some codes require all junctions be made inside a junction box. This is especially true where conduit is required. If nonmetallic cable is banned in your area, the use of conduit and its accessories is described at the end of this chapter. The following instructions apply to either.

*VI-5*

**VI-5.** The picture shows steps in making a splice. Remove about three inches of insulation from each wire with a pocketknife or a multipurpose wiring tool. Next cross wires at midpoint as you use pliers and fingers to wrap them tightly in opposite directions. Stagger joints. Do not make joints on parallel wires opposite each other. Using soldering paste designed for soldering copper, lightly coat joint area of bare wires. Now heat with a torch as you apply a thin coat of solder. Finish job by wrapping joint with electrician's tape.

*VI-6*

**VI-6.** Here is how to make a tap. When you have removed the insulation, as shown, and wrapped the bare end of one wire several times around the bare area of the tapped wire, solder and wrap joint with electrician's plastic tape similar to above instructions for wrapping the splice.

*VI-7*

**VI-7.** Make connection at screw terminals by removing ¾ inch of insulation from end of wire. With long-nose pliers, bend bare end of wire clockwise to fit around screw. Tightening screw tends to hold end of wire firmly against screw; wires bent counterclockwise tend to pull away from screw as it is tightened.

Keep these 5 principles in mind as you install the circuits:

1. Attach hot wires (black or red) directly to switches;
2. Attach neutral wires (white) to current-consuming devices, such as lights and motors;
3. Attach ground wire (bare or covered green) to metal, such as outlet, switch, or light metal box;
4. Attach hot wires to brass-colored termi-

nals; neutral wires to light or silver-colored terminals;
5. Join black wires to black wires, red wires to red wires, and white wires to white wires continuously throughout the circuits. The only exception is at switch loops where ends of white wires are taped or painted black to denote hot lines.

*VI-8*

**VI-8.** A single-pole switch is used to control one or more fixtures from a single point.

*VI-9*

**VI-9.** Two three-way switches are used to control one or more fixtures from two different points.

**VI-10.** A four-way switch is used between two three-way switches to control one or more fixtures from three different points. You can control one or more fixtures from as many different points as you please by connecting as many additional four-way switches as you have control points between the four-way switch (just de-

VI-10

scribed) and either one of the three-way switches. Suppose you want to control a fixture from ten different points. Your hook-up would require light four-way switches installed between two three-way switches.

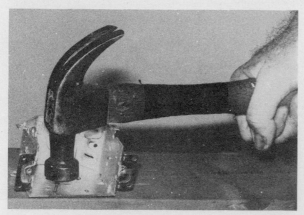

VI-11

**VI-11.** Begin with the service outlet box installations. Using two 1-inch round-head screws or 1½-inch corrugated nails, fasten metal box hangers to wood framework. For easy installation, temporarily remove one side plate of box.

Switch outlet boxes are installed in the same way as the service outlet boxes.

If your greenhouse walls are of concrete blocks, your service outlet and switch cables should extend out of openings, as recommended in Chapter IV. If this is not the case, refer to the suggested installations before proceeding. Cables can also be strung along the greenhouse framework. Fasten them in place with metal straps held by 1-inch roofing nails.

**VI-12.** Using two 1-inch round-head screws or one ½-inch corrugated nails, fasten overhead light service boxes to ceiling joist or rafter.

If your plans call for junction boxes, install

VI-12

them at this time. (Note: These boxes are the same as those used for ceiling lights.) Later, when bare ends of wires inside are twisted together and insulated, either with solderless connectors or electrician's plastic tape, use screw to fasten flat metal cover (made for the purpose) onto open end of box.

VI-13

**VI-13.** Now you are ready to wire the 115-volt service outlet circuit. *Caution:* Be sure power is not connected to service panel. Remove ½ inch of insulation from black and white wires, as well as enough cable covering to make service panel connections. Fasten white wire and bare ground wire to neutral strip in service panel. Then fasten black wire to a single circuit breaker—after snapping in place on service panel—of correct amperage for circuit. If cable has not been previously brought to outlet box, do it now. Bring cable to approximately 1 foot beyond first outlet box, fastening to framework every 4½ feet with staples designed for fastening nonmetallic cable. Then make cut forming two cable ends. Trim about 8 inches of cover from each of the two cables with a sharp pocketknife. Be sure not to damage insulation on wires. Then string each cable through a knockout hole after removing two knockouts from box. Each outlet box—with exception of last box in circuit—has an incoming and an outgoing cable. Tighten clamps inside box with a screwdriver, holding cables firmly in place. Fasten ground wire from each cable with screw to an unused hole in box.

Strip about ¾ inch of insulation from each of the four wires with a multipurpose tool or pocketknife. Then connect black wires to copper-colored terminals, white wires to silver-colored terminals on the service outlet. Now position outlet to box with wires pushed inside. Then, using the two screws packaged with outlet, fasten it securely to box.

*VI-14*

**VI-14.** Install overhead lights on a separate circuit. Fasten cable wires at service panel, stringing and fastening cable to each light outlet box, and extending, cutting, and fastening cable wires to box as described above for wiring the service outlet circuit, with this exception: A shows the hot line or incoming feed cable. B shows control

cable running from light outlet box to single-pole switch. C shows outgoing feed cable from outlet box to next light outlet box in the circuit. Twist together black wire from feed cable A, black wire from switch cable B, and black wire from feed cable C. Paint black or tape end of white wire in switch cable as well as end of white wire at the switch location. (Note: Always blacken both ends of switch wires if not already black. This denotes line is hot and not neutral.) Now twist together white wires of incoming feed cable A and outgoing feed cable C. Also, use a screw to fasten the three ground wires to the metal box.

Wire remaining boxes in light circuit. Then mount light fixtures of your choice to each box, after twisting bare end of black wire (switch wire) to bare end of single black wire in box, bare end of white wire to twisted white wires in box, and green wire (ground) to previously fastened ground wires inside box. Insulate bare ends of insulated wires in box either with solderless connectors or plastic electrician's tape.

Wiring of light circuit is complete after you connect the two black ends of switch cable wires to a single-pole switch and ground wire to inside of metal switch box. With wires pushed back into box, use the two screws packaged with switch to fasten it to box. With the single-pole switch you can turn the light on and off from only one point. If you wish to control a light from more than one location, use three- and four-way switches—as described and illustrated earlier in this chapter.

**VI-15.** Complete service outlet and light cir-

*VI-15*

cuits by fastening proper cover plates onto service outlets and switches. Use screws packaged with the plates.

## Installation Of Low Voltage Circuits

Some of your equipment may show low-voltage circuits of 24 volts. Generally, instructions accompanying such equipment include wiring diagrams and one or more transformers, which are used in reducing a 115-volt circuit to 24 volts. One side of a transformer contains terminals for making connections to a 115-volt circuit, while the opposite side contains terminals for connecting to low-voltage devices, such as timers and electric water valves. Here different colored bell wire is used for making the connections, while wire previously recommended for 115-volt circuits is used for connecting the transformer to the 115-volt circuit.

## Installation Of Electric Motors

Provide separate circuits for any electric motor equipment you plan to use. Be sure to follow information on the electric motor nameplate, where you will also find the model and serial numbers. These are required when contacting the manufacturer for replacement, repairs, or general information.

The name plate also shows the current necessary for safe operation. Sixty-cycle alternating current (AC) is required for most motors. Without going into technical details, motors with a smaller capacity are manufactured to use a one-phase current; some require 115 volts, while others require 230 volts. Generally, larger motors use 230 volts and may be either one phase or three phase. These differences in design should not cause problems in wiring. Circuits—with the exception of low-voltage circuits—previously described are on single-phase current. This is the common current found in most home and farm wiring; only single-phase motors should be connected to it. Three-phase circuits are commonly found in industrial wiring, such as in factories, and three-phase motors are designed for connecting to them. Incidentally, three-phase motors are smaller, less expensive to manufacture, and much simpler in design than single-phase motors. It is unlikely that the average residence can be sup-plied with three-phase power, but be sure to use three-phase motors—of large capacity—if it is available. To be on the safe side, always follow the wiring diagrams included on the motor nameplate and/or the instruction leaflet. Double check that you receive the instruction leaflet from your supplier, because it also contains maintenance suggestions for the motor, such as whether to oil or *not*. All motors require free air circulation around them.

Most motors today use V belts and pulleys to transmit power to electrical equipment. Belts and pulleys have a way of wearing out, but the replacement data will be on them. Even though the numbers may be obliterated, come replacement time, take the worn pieces to your electric supplier, who can offer duplicates. When you make the replacements, be sure pulleys are tight on the shafts, and the belt between pulleys is tight enough not to slip but not tight enough to smoke when the motor is in operation. In short, belts need only be tight enough to furnish the right amount of friction between them and the pulleys so that the motor operates freely without being under strain.

Once the motor specifications are understood, use the following table to determine maximum amperage to be carried by the motor cable wires.

### Amperage Requirements of Motors of Different Horsepower

| Motor horsepower | 115-volt amperes required | 230-volt amperes required |
|---|---|---|
| ¼ | 6 | 3 |
| ⅓ | 7 | 3½ |
| ½ | 10 | 5 |
| ¾ | 14 | 7 |
| 1 | 16 | 8 |
| 1½ | 20 | 10 |
| 2 | 24 | 12 |

Now that you have the total amperage required with respect to the motors, 115 and 230 volt, determine correct wire size for the circuits from wire size tables previously shown in this chapter, one for 115 volts, the other for 230 volts. Selecting wire size for motors is different from selecting wire size for other electrical devices, such as lights, for example. Motors consume more amperage in the process of reaching full speed than they do when full speed is reached. Therefore, select wires large enough to supply required voltage for both starting the motor as well as for running it at full speed. Generally, if wires are selected to supply required voltage when motor is running at full speed only, there will be a drop of voltage during the starting period of approximately 3-7 percent, depending on such factors as type of motor and how hard the load is to get underway.

As mentioned before, many of the smaller motors operate on 115 volts. However, if you have a motor or other equipment operating on 230 volts, install a 230-volt circuit breaker, amperage size to match wire size, in service panel. Connect black and red wires (hot wires) to circuit breaker and ground wire to neutral strip in service panel.

Then run cable, fastened every 4½ feet with metal straps, from service panel to outlet box, where you install a 230-volt service outlet, mounted to a metal service box, to accept the 230-volt male plug on end of cord from the motor. Sometimes, the terminals are located on the motor for accepting the cable wires directly. In this case, a service outlet box and service outlet are not required. (Note: For safety, ground all electric motors, no matter how small their size.)

### Wiring With Thin-Wall Conduit

The principles of wiring for laying out and installing the circuits for service outlets, switches, lights, and motors are the same whether you use nonmetallic cable, as described previously, or thin-wall conduit. Therefore, the installation techniques applying specifically to thin-wall conduit follow.

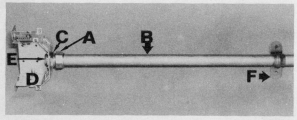

*VI-16*

**VI-16.** The picture shows a hookup for a service outlet. Thin-wall conduit—also called electrical metal tubing or Type EMT—is used. (Note: One side of service outlet box is removed for clarity.)

Begin by fitting threadless end of connector A over conduit B, tighten compression nut C. Now insert threaded end through knockout (following removal of knockout) of box D. Then screw locknut E (tooth side faces box) tightly against box from the inside. Support conduit with pipe straps F. Use a coupling to join two lengths of conduit together.

Keep in mind these eight cardinal principles as you install thin-wall conduit:

1.    Thin-wall conduit can be placed indoors or outdoors. However, you should not use it either in cinder block construction or buried in cinders.

2.    No ground wire is required in the circuits, since metal conduit and metal boxes provide a continuous ground.

3.    Select correct size of conduit—which comes in 10-foot lengths—from the following table:

**Conduit Size with Relationship to Size and Number of Wires**

| Wire Size | Number of Wires to be Installed | | | | | |
|---|---|---|---|---|---|---|
| | 1 | 2 | 3 | 4 | 5 | 6 |
| | *Size of Conduit in Inches* | | | | | |
| 14 | ½ | ½ | ½ | ½ | ¾ | ¾ |
| 12 | ½ | ½ | ½ | ¾ | ¾ | 1 |
| 10 | ½ | ¾ | ¾ | ¾ | 1 | 1 |
| 8 | ½ | ¾ | ¾ | 1 | 1¼ | 1¼ |
| 6 | ½ | 1 | 1 | 1¼ | 1½ | 1½ |
| 4 | ½ | 1¼ | 1¼ | 1½ | 1½ | 2 |
| 2 | ¾ | 1¼ | 1¼ | 2 | 2 | 2 |
| 1/0 | 1 | 1½ | 2 | 2 | 2½ | 2½ |
| 2/0 | 1 | 2 | 2 | 2½ | 2½ | 3 |
| 3/0 | 1 | 2 | 2 | 2½ | 3 | 3 |

4.    Use a hacksaw (blade with 32 teeth per inch) to cut conduit, then ream inside, rough edge with a file.

**VI-17.**    5.    Use a conduit bender as shown in the picture for bending conduit. This is an inexpensive tool that you can purchase from most hardware stores or electrical shops. Also, you can rent one from a tool rental service. Bend gradually, keeping in mind that if bend continued to form a circle, it would equal at least 12 times

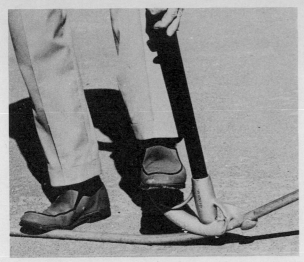

*VI-17*

are experienced, I advise bending conduit first, then cutting. Also, fasten boxes temporarily in place so they can be moved slightly if cuts or bends are not quite up to measurements.

6. Anchor conduit to surface with a pipe strap, 3 feet from each metal box, 6 feet thereafter on exposed runs, and every 10 feet on concealed runs.

7. Make splices and taps inside metal boxes. Splice must never be inside conduit itself.

8. Following installation of conduit and boxes, pull wires through conduit into boxes. You can probably push a few small wires in at one end on through to next outlet, if run is not too long. For long runs, especially if there are bends, use a fish wire. This is a steel tape approximately ⅛-inch wide, in lengths of either 50 or 100 feet. It is especially designed for pulling wires through conduit and may be purchased from your local electric supply house.

the inside diameter of the conduit. Use factory-bent elbows for bending large sizes. Unless you

VII-1.   Partitions and the proper equipment make it possible to divide a greenhouse into cool, warm, and/or tropical compartments or sections.

# VII

# Heating

In all but a few localities, heating the greenhouse during fall, winter, and spring months is essential for proper plant growth if the greenhouse is to be operated on a 12-months basis. Your choice of a heating system and accessory equipment is one of the most important steps in greenhouse construction. The installation of some heating systems can be an expensive item, especially if you must have the work done. However, other heating systems are designed for the amateur to install. This reduces the installation cost drastically. Although space does not permit a complete treatment on how to install the many varied heating systems on the market, this chapter offers suggestions for making a good selection. At the same time, it points out ways to keep heating installations costs to a minimum.

## SPECIES OF PLANTS

As noted in Chapter I, plants have rather definite temperature requirements for maximum growth. So keep in mind whether the heating system is to provide adequate heat for a cool, warm, or tropical climate, or a combination of all three types. Generally, daytime temperatures on sunny days are maintained 10-15° higher than night temperatures. On cloudy days temperatures are required 5-10° lower than on sunny days. These are only general temperature variations. Perhaps some of the plants you wish to grow will do better at slightly varying temperatures. Since this book does not attempt to treat greenhouse gardening as such, one or more of the references in the Appendix provide information on specific requirements, including recommended temperatures, for different plant species.

## SIZE OF HEATING SYSTEM

Since most heating systems state their output rating in British thermal units (BTUs), you should know the BTU requirements for your particular greenhouse. These ten guidelines indicate why greenhouses of the same size may require vastly different heating systems:

1. The minimum inside temperature desired.
2. The lowest anticipated outside temperature.
3. Amount of exposure to winds.
4. Nature of the greenhouse surface area.
5. Double or single layering of sidewalls.
6. Double or single glazed greenhouse.
7. Amount of straw or other material used to cover roof (not to the point of blocking out too much sunlight) during extremely cold weather.
8. Desirability of maintaining maximum temperatures during extreme periods of cold weather.
9. Attachment of greenhouse to heated building (as with a lean-to greenhouse).
10. Excellent, good, or poor operating and maintenance schedule.

A rule of thumb for estimating the safety margin for most greenhouses is a heat loss of 1.2 BTUs per hour for each degree of temperature differential (difference between inside and outside temperature) per square foot of exposed surface. Heating requirements for most greenhouses can be calculated from the following chart:

### Greenhouse Heating Requirements*

| Desired minimal inside temperature | Lowest outside temperature | | | | | |
|---|---|---|---|---|---|---|
| | 20°F | 10°F | 0°F | −10°F | −20°F | −30°F |
| F | BTUs required per hour per square foot of exposed surface. | | | | | |
| 50° | 36 | 48 | 60 | 72 | 84 | 96 |
| 55° | 42 | 54 | 66 | 78 | 90 | 102 |
| 60° | 48 | 60 | 72 | 84 | 96 | 108 |
| 65° | 54 | 66 | 78 | 90 | 102 | 114 |
| 70° | 60 | 72 | 84 | 96 | 108 | 120 |

* Figure total heat requirement for your greenhouse by multiplying the BTUs required per square foot (see table) times the total square feet of exposed greenhouse surface. For example, to maintain a 60° temperature inside a 10 x 18-foot greenhouse with 618 feet of exposed wall and roof surface, when the outside temperature is −10°F., a heater with an output of 52,000 BTUs is required. As a margin of safety, these requirements should be increased by a minimum of 10 percent.

When you arrive at the greenhouse BTU requirements, select a heating system which is equal to at least 10 percent more than required, as suggested in footnote to the table. There is far less wear and tear if the capacity is a little larger than actually required. Then, too, if you encounter a record-breaking year with low temperatures, the heating system will carry you through. Even though greenhouse plants are not directly exposed to outside temperatures, they can be lost if the weather is unusually cold and your heating system is adequate only for seasonal temperatures.

## HEATING THE GREENHOUSE

Regardless of the kind of heating system you install in the greenhouse, it is only a vehicle or a means to an end. The job at hand is to heat the air, in spite of outside temperatures, and maintain that heat at a desired temperature. The right heating system depends upon size and construction of the greenhouse, initial cost, fuel available, economy of operation, and how much, if any, of the installation you can do.

Since fuel oil, electricity, natural gas, bottle gas, or coal are all satisfactory fuels for use in greenhouse heating, choose the one most likely to be available during the heating season. Low operating cost is another factor to consider in selecting a fuel. If coal is the desirable fuel, give thought to installing a heating system producing a minimum amount of air pollution. Even though you may not have restrictions now, this may change in the future. Once installed, a change of systems can be costly and time-consuming.

### Extension Of The Home Heating System

If the BTU capacity of your home heating system is large enough to heat only your home, do not burden it by also trying to heat the greenhouse with it. On the other hand, if the system is oversized, there is no reason why you cannot extend it to the greenhouse. This is particularly true if the greenhouse is small or is attached to the home.

Unless you are a heating expert, secure advice from a heating contractor, mail-order house, or a greenhouse supplier about installing an additional zone for heating the greenhouse. Generally, this is not an expensive job to do with hot water or steam systems. It is a simple matter of extending the heating pipes to the greenhouse. For hot air systems, cold and warm air ducts can be extended into the greenhouse, providing it is not located too far from the home. With either of the three systems, a thermostat located in the greenhouse can control temperatures without interfering with the home heating requirements. Locate the thermometer at plant growing height and not for your own convenience. It is best to use alcohol-filled thermometers. Thermometers filled with mercury will damage certain plants, such as roses, with vapors given off when broken.

### Convection Heaters

A convection heater works this way: As cold, dense layers of air drift downward they push the warm (heated air), less dense layers upward. Or, putting it another way, as heated layers of air rise and cold layers of air sink, a convection current is set up which continues as long as both hot and cold layers of air come in contact with each other. (Note: In addition to the hot air furnace, the hot water and steam furnace with radiators heats the air almost entirely by convection.)

*VII-2.  Portable heaters, such as kerosene heater A, gasoline catalytic heater B (also available with propane as a fuel), and electric heater C, can provide the greenhouse with heat supplement during extremely cold weather.*

The advantages of convection heaters are: 1) ease of installation; and 2) use of a clean fuel such as bottled or natural gas. Many such heaters are used satisfactorily, but they are not as efficient at circulating heat as warm air heaters equipped with a blower system. If you plan on building a plastic-covered greenhouse, they have another disadvantage. In such houses, warm-air convection heaters produce less uniform temperature and higher humidity than forced warm-air heaters. This results in more condensation of moisture, which works hand in glove in producing diseased plants. *Warning:* Never use an unvented fuel-burning heater in a greenhouse. The risk of someone being overcome with carbon monoxide is much, much too great—to say nothing of the bad effect it will have on your plants! Carbon monoxide is given off from incomplete combustion, as well as other gases, such as ethylene, which are harmful to plants.

If you plan to use a warm-air convection heater, install either a 4- or 6-inch (depending upon the size of the flue collar) stovepipe vent system around the perimeter of the building. Since the system is based on the principle of hot air rising because it is lighter than cold air, locate vent pipes close to floor. As the products of combustion form, they pass through the vent system around the inside of the greenhouse and finally travel up the chimney to the outside. As the circulation takes place, heat from the pipes warms the air.

**Forced Warm-Air Heaters**

You can use the same kind of forced warm-air heater for the greenhouse that is used in residential heating. If the greenhouse is large, heating ducts provide a more efficient system. Forced warm-air heaters come in different designs. Some are horizontal and fit nicely out of the way under a bench. Others are taller and can be kept completely out of the way by installing them in an adjoining building, such as a garage, attached to the greenhouse. With such installations the heat is distributed throughout the greenhouse by a duct system and a fan.

**Boilers**

High-efficiency, self-contained hot water or steam boilers fitted with burners for using oil, gas, or oil-gas combination are considered by many greenhouse gardeners the most satisfactory type of heating system. Although the initial cost is high, the installation cost can be low. This is possible because with many of the systems, the factory installs, wires, and tests the parts before shipping. Heat is distributed in the greenhouse by means of metal fin radiation heaters or unit heaters, and anyone handy with tools can install them after reading the instructions accompanying the package deal. When gardeners install two or more temperature zones, they prefer a hot water

*VII-3. No usable greenhouse space lost here, boiler is located in attached building. Boiler is also large enough to heat the home, so mess and pump noise is away from living quarters.*

system over that of steam. However, do not overlook the fact that steam from a steam boiler can be used to sterilize (pasteurize) greenhouse soil.

### Small Heaters

Small oil, gas, or electric heaters are becoming more and more popular for heating greenhouses. They are easy to install, the least expensive, clean and efficient; the electric heaters do not need a venting system. Also, their compactness takes little valuable greenhouse space. All you do with an electric heater is connect it to a separate 230-volt circuit, with circuit breaker, in service panel sized according to instructions accompanying package. *Caution:* Before making installation, see Chapter VI. With a gas heater, provide a vent system and connect motor to branch circuit in accordance with instructions inside package.

*VII-4. This heater (sizes vary between 250,000 and 500,000 BTUs) was use-tested before shipment and completely portable. It gives clean, safe heat, and is designed for years of troublefree, economical, maintenance-free service.*

*VII-5. This gas heater is thermostatically controlled, easily installed, fully vented, and completely automatic. Models vary in size, making it ideal for the small greenhouse. It is also practical in larger greenhouses, where two or more heaters can be used to produce the required number of BTUs.*

Use electric heating cable for better propagation and uniform plant production. The uniform heat of electric soil heating cable far surpasses the inconsistency of manure hotbeds. Plants grow rapidly and uniformly throughout the bed. Growth can be governed accurately since heat is thermostatically controlled. The automatic operation assures less "damping off," "seeding," and root rot. It also saves work and cuts power costs. Heating cable can be used in hotbeds, cold frames, or greenhouse benches. Put the heat where it is needed by burying cable about six inches in the soil.

See catalog instructions with regard to number of feet required to take care of the square footage in your hotbed. Also, see Chapter X. By connecting cables in parallel, you can heat beds of any size. Heating cables have many other applications around the greenhouse and the home, such as preventing ice to form on gutters, eaves, and downspouts. They can be used to protect water pipes from freezing and to melt ice on driveways and walks. As one can surmise, heating cables have many, many uses, but one thing they are not designed for is actual greenhouse heating.

## SOME FINAL THOUGHTS ON HEATING

Consider these guidelines while planning the greenhouse heating system:

1.   Choose a heater that is automatic in operation and requires minimum maintenance.

2.   Select a heater large enough to heat the greenhouse. Check with your local weather bureau to find out the coldest day during the past twenty-five years. Use the lowest temperature as a criterion when establishing BTU requirements for a heating system to do the job.

3.   A windy location results in a greater heat loss, so provide a windbreak as previously described to help cut heating costs; otherwise order a heater one size larger than necessary.

4.   When installing a central heating system, give thought to additional capacity if you plan to add a workshop later, enlarge the greenhouse, or have one plant heat greenhouse and home.

5.   Take heed when using any type of vented heater. Use every precaution to prevent downdrafts. One cause for downdrafts can be that the top of the chimney is not high enough to clear ridge of greenhouse or nearby building at least two feet. Other causes may be drafts coming through open doors of adjoining buildings or open roof ventilators in the greenhouse. Keep all doors and roof vents closed when the heating system is in operation. Not only will downdrafts be reduced but the heating costs will be cheaper. From a health point of view, downdrafts can be harmful to plants, humans, and animals.

6.   Never use a heating system that requires

manufactured gas as a fuel, it is injurious to plants.

7.   Be certain heating system is equipped with adequate controls, such as safety pilots and an automatic shutoff switch.

8.   Locate several accurate thermostats, positioned at plant height, throughout the greenhouse to provide a check on heat distribution.

9.   Place shades above thermometers and thermostats to avoid false readings caused by sun rays.

10.   Install a temperature alarm to warn of dangerously low temperatures. Be sure to set temperature warning high enough to give time to remedy heating or power failure before plants are killed.

11.   Provide for emergency heat. Position portable kerosene heaters and/or gasolene or propane catalytic heaters throughout the greenhouse. Perhaps a better way is to install a stand-by electric generator of sufficient wattage to meet power failure or brownouts. Fueled either with gasolene or diesel fuel, these generators can be purchased either of a size to furnish just lighting and run furnace motors, or large enough to operate stand-by electric heaters as well as supply an emergency number of watts for your home.

12.   Some of the less complicated heating systems are as simple to install as connecting a service outlet cable to the terminals on an electric motor or heater. Other systems are not necessarily complicated to install, the problem lies in the fact that they all differ. Obviously, it is not possible to outline the installation procedures for the many varying systems on the market today. Rather, I recommend taking advantage of the free engineering service offered by a number of greenhouse manufacturers: explicit instructions, specifically written for the heating system you choose for your greenhouse conditions. Generally, upon request, manufacturers send the customer a questionnaire for securing greenhouse information. From this information, optimum heating plant service can be planned.

# VIII

# Ventilating, Cooling, and Humidifying

The efficiency of plant growth inside a greenhouse depends to a large extent on a suitable atmospheric environment, carefully adjusted during the day and night to suit needs of the plants. A suitable environment has several salient elements: air supply, air distribution, air cooling or control of temperature, and humidity control.

This chapter notes general considerations involved in setting up a suitable atmospheric environment as it applies to ventilating, cooling, and humidifying.

## VENTILATING

Whether building a greenhouse yourself or selecting one already constructed, give special attention to the design and the way in which it is ventilated, since ventilation and temperature are key issues in greenhouse management. In fact, a close relationship exists between ventilation and temperature. No matter how small the greenhouse, there should be some provision made for ventilation at the highest point, usually near the ridge of the roof, where hot air rises to collect. The best arrangement for good ventilation is to alternate the vents on each side of the roof adjoining the ridge. This is not necessary for small greenhouses where there is only need for one roof vent. Vents should be built into the vertical sides of the greenhouse either at or below bench level. The purpose is to supply incoming fresh air. The combination of ridge vents and side vents provide desirable air currents inside the greenhouse.

Every ventilation system should meet these objectives:

1. To exchange inside air for fresh outside air. Such an exchange is just as important for plants as it is for people when several are closed up hour after hour in an unventilated room. Fresh air has a way of ventilizing plants and improving their living processes.

2. To control temperatures by allowing hot air to escape from a high point, to be replaced by cooler, fresh air entering at a lower level.

3. To be able to exchange air of high humidity, caused by plant transpiration, with fresh, drier air which is capable of absorbing more moisture.

4. To insure against attacks from plant diseases and pests, which are more prevalent in unventilated quarters.

### Hand-Powered Ventilators

Square or rectangular roof vents are the traditional methods of ventilating greenhouses. Generally, one edge is hinged to the roof adjoining the ridge, and the opposite or lower edge is held in place with hand-operated fasteners or mechanical vent-lifting equipment. If possible, locate your greenhouse at right angle to prevailing winds. This provides for flexibility for ridge vent operation. Where only one ridge vent is provided, as in basement-entrance or lean-to models, locate vent away from prevailing winds to prevent cold air from blowing directly on the plants during cold-weather ventilation.

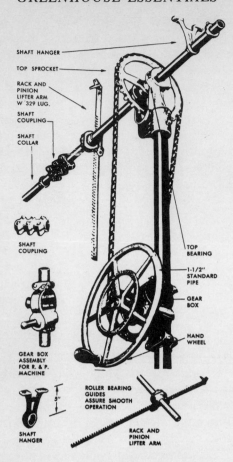

SHAFT HANGER
TOP SPROCKET
RACK AND PINION LIFTER ARM W 329 LUG.
SHAFT COUPLING
SHAFT COLLAR

SHAFT COUPLING

GEAR BOX ASSEMBLY FOR R. & P. MACHINE

SHAFT HANGER

TOP BEARING
1-1/2" STANDARD PIPE
GEAR BOX
HAND WHEEL

ROLLER BEARING GUIDES ASSURE SMOOTH OPERATION

RACK AND PINION LIFTER ARM

*VIII-1*

**VIII-1.** Mechanical vent-lifting speeds up the operation of long runs of roof ventilators. You can use chain-pull vent machines on short runs of roof ventilators. For average runs of, say 75 or even 100 feet, a worm and gear vent machine equipped with hand wheel does an effective job of opening and closing vents. If your runs are longer, say up to 150 feet, use a rack and pinion vent machine equipped with a hand wheel as shown in the picture. This one is supplied by The National Greenhouse Company.

As mentioned before, side vents are a necessary part of any greenhouse as a means of providing proper ventilation. Locate foundation vents as part of the side wall, so that incoming air passes under the benches, preventing drafts from blowing directly on the plants. If drafts persist, make a deflector from a piece of light galvanized iron sheeting. Bend and fasten it with nails or screws in such a way as to deflect incoming air from striking plants directly. Another way to control incoming air drafts is to install jalousie vents in end walls. Sometimes two are used, one at each end of the greenhouse, to provide

cross ventilation. For more effective ventilation, substitute an exhaust fan for one of the jalousies.

If your plans call for a small greenhouse, use a storm door; the screened section can serve the ventilation purpose. In any event, do not use unscreened openings for ventilation purposes unless you wish to provide a sanctuary for insects and birds.

### Mechanical Ventilators

For the reader who has little time, or who does not care for hand-operated vent lifting equipment —or who just desires better temperature control —an automatic, motorized vent system should be considered.

*VIII-2*

**VIII-2.** There are many automatic vent control systems on the market today. The one shown in the picture is manufactured by The National Greenhouse Company. It makes use of a specially designed motor which turns at a slow speed, assuring a quiet operation. Even temperature control takes place because the vents open extremely slowly. Often, this satisfies the thermostat so rapidly that vents begin to close without having gone all the way open. There are no belts to get out of adjustment or slip. As vents close tight on mounting frame header, motor shuts off automatically. Vents can be held open at any desired position. Second to automatic ventilation systems is ventilating by thermostatically controlled exhaust fans. Exhaust fans are practical, realistic, and easy to install. They provide positive ventilation in both large and small greenhouses. Use one or more fans so there is a complete change of air every minute during warm weather. Select a fan that has two speeds and is rubber-mounted with sealed ball bearings for long life. Also, fan shutters should be fully automatic so that they open when fan turns on and close when it shuts off.

## COOLING

Adequate ventilation provides some cooling for the greenhouse, generally not enough for profitable, comfortable gardening. Additional cooling is helpful during hot weather. Think about the following questions—which all need yes answers —when planning your cooling system, whether it is a combination of hand-operated venting devices and a simple shading, or a sophisticated shading program plus mechanical cooling:

1.  Will it lower the temperature 10-20 degrees during hot weather?
2.  Will it eliminate the need for shutting down the greenhouse during hot weather (related to 1.)?
3.  Is it possible to raise top quality crops year round?
4.  Will it reduce, slightly, the amount of water plants require?
5.  Will it provide filtered, moist air (which is vital for quality plant production)?
6.  Will it and the ventilating system eliminate stagnant air?
7.  Will it aid in keeping plants on a sound growing schedule?
8.  Will the temperature be comfortable, for employee and customer comfort, if they are inside the greenhouse?

### Shading

The temperature inside the greenhouse can be reduced by a good shading system. The greenhouse gardener will find this most advantageous in his operational program. Shading, coupled with moisture from wet soil or from a humidifier, will sometimes lower temperatures as much as 15°. Shading has little effect, if any, on plant growth, because summer sunlight is generally in excess of its requirements.

Slat, roll-up shades installed on outside of greenhouse provide cooling of inside temperature. An evaporative cooling system installed outside the greenhouse adds to temperature reduction by pulling in fresh air through wet pads.

Shading can be provided by painting or spraying specially formulated compounds on the glass: either a concentrated material that only needs water added for immediate application, or a powder, ready to mix with water and use immediately. Generally, the shading materials can be removed with a brush or hose, yet they remain on through a rain.

Follow these guidelines to select a satisfactory shading compound:

1.  All additives should be included, so that a fixative is not required.
2.  Density should be easy to regulate.
3.  Materials should remain in suspension and not settle.
4.  Material should be ready to use after mixing. Avoid any with a wetting-down period.
5.  If material stands for days, it should not sour if kept agitated.
6.  *Caution:* Do not use shading materials containing lime, clay, or flour. Such ingredients have a tendency to rot paint and putty, which will cause leaks; lime is not good for metal framing.

Shading cloth offers several advantages over other shade materials:

1.  Uniform shade, rather than a pattern of dark and light areas, is given.
2.  A specific weight that will provide exact degree of shade required can be purchased.
3.  Cloth is fireproof—melts in flame but will not burn.
4.  It provides hail protection, breaks driving rain, and eliminates drip.
5.  Heat is held in by cloth when heaters are in use.
6.  It is light in weight, thus requiring few support posts.
7.  A goodly number of insects are kept out of the greenhouse by cloth.

*VIII-3.   You can cut wood wheels and countersink bolt or screw holes (so that head of bolt or screw will not catch cloth) to fasten on shading cloth frames, or you can purchase them from most greenhouse suppliers.*

## EVAPORATIVE

### Cooling

An air-conditioning system should be installed to grow cool greenhouse plants or for maximum growth of warm greenhouse plants during the hot weather season. (Note: Compressor-type air conditioners, such as used in homes and places of business, are not realistic for cooling greenhouses.) The only practical way to cool a greenhouse as much as 15-25° is through evaporative cooling units. Such units cool the warm, fresh air as it is drawn from the outside through wet filter pads by a strong fan or blower and injected into the greenhouse.

**VIII-4.** The picture shows an evaporative cooler. It is easy to install and gives many years of quiet, smooth running, trouble-free performance. A powerful fan draws hot, dry, outside air through a thick moistened pad, which cools the air, and on through a duct to the inside of the greenhouse.

**VIII-5.** The National Greenhouse Company supplies a fan jet convection ventilation system. This is a multipurpose ventilating and cooling system. It is moderately priced, easy to install, and does a superior job of improving growing conditions in a greenhouse. The fan on the unit runs continuously, taking air from inside the greenhouse and recirculating it. When the greenhouse heats up excessively, the thermostat starts the exhaust fan, which pulls a slight vacuum in the house. At the same time, a motorized shutter on the fan jet opens and the cool, fresh outside air "jumps" across to the tube and is evenly distributed throughout the greenhouse.

*VIII-4*

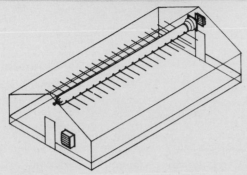

*VIII-5*

**VIII-6.** Automatic mist propagation systems are used for intermittent misting of cuttings such as poinsettias, mums, and certain varieties of nursery stock because of their tremendous value in rooting. Wilt is kept to a minimum because the exact amount of mist can be controlled twenty-four hours a day.

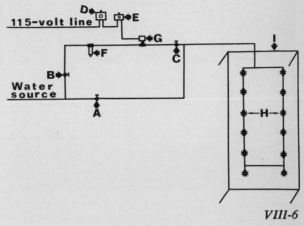

*VIII-6*

## HUMIDIFYING

Regulated humidity in the greenhouse promotes rich, thick foliage with all plants. Small greenhouse operators find frequent wetting down of the floor, crushed rock under benches, and walks an effective and inexpensive method of increasing humidity. Plants, such as orchids and tropical foliage plants, grow best in high humidity. For these special purposes, even for the small greenhouse, automatic unit humidifiers are available at prices to suit almost any budget.

The kind of mist propagation system I recommend works something like the one in the diagram. With shutoff valve A closed and shutoff valves B and C open, the system works automatically. For example, setting 24-hour timer D to operate between 8:00 A.M. and 4:00 P.M. causes minute timer E to activate solenoid valve G, causing water to reach Florida nozzles H (located on raised bench I) six seconds, say, out of each minute—if this is the setting desired for the minute timer. In case of power failure or electrical difficulties within the misting system, the opening of shutoff valve A and the closing of shutoff valves B and C prepare the system for hand operation. F is a water line strainer.

# IX

# Equipment

Before discussing how to construct different greenhouses in the following chapters, I want to present information on general equipment, so that you can build your model large enough to house the equipment you feel is necessary to meet your gardening requirements or plan additions on an existing building to house some of it. Since basic equipment dealing with heating, ventilating, cooling and humidification was discussed previously, this section will deal with other kinds of equipment desirable for successful greenhouse gardening.

An important consideration is the relationship of greenhouse equipment to the requirements of the plants. The construction of a greenhouse requires basic tools and technical know-how. The construction of your greenhouse garden demands those same things: basic tools—the equipment—and know-how. Since the greenhouse equipment is a vital part of your gardening tools, buy the best that your budget permits. Since the techniques of plant behavior is not an intended part of this book, reference materials are given in the Appendix for those readers who wish to broaden their knowledge in this area. Nonetheless, every gardener can add to his skill by having his greenhouse properly equipped. The right piece of equipment at the right time not only helps him to do a better job of raising plants, but it makes the work smoother and faster, and working conditions pleasant.

## WATER STORAGE TANKS

Because an abundant supply of water is essential to greenhouse gardening, there should be adequate storage, as well as a supply of tap water for additional use. There are at least two good arguments for storing water: 1. Rain water is softer than tap water, and it is free of manmade chemicals. 2. Even tap water, when stored in a tank, is at a temperature more acceptable to plants.

Take advantage of available rain water by guttering the greenhouse; the gutters should slope slightly toward end of house nearest tank. Use downspout to lead water from gutter through wall, thence into tank. Most mail-order firms not only supply guttering parts but furnish instructions for the installer's convenience. (Note: Do not run water from roof coated with a shading compound which is solubilized or which runs off in the rain water, since this could effect pH of soil or cause increased soluble salts on plants watered with it.)

Size of operation and space allotted determine quantity of water stored. Although your requirements actually determine amount of water stored, it is a good idea to consider a tank or tanks, each with a capacity of approximately 100 gallons. Not only is one huge tank impractical for a large operation, but it is less functional than having one or more smaller tanks located in different areas of the greenhouse. For instance, two 100-gallon tanks, one at each end of the greenhouse, would be more practical than one huge tank centrally located.

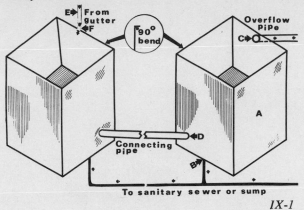

*IX-1*

**IX-1.** Sheet metal work takes experience. If you have not handled this before, have your local tinner make the tank assembly with the following parts:

A. 3 x 3 x 4 feet deep (or size to suit) x #18 gauge galvanized iron tank. Tank is more rigid if ⅝ inch of top edge is bent at a 90° angle, as shown in detail in the picture.

B. ½-inch drain connection—used as a cleanout when maintenance time rolls around, as well as to drain water from tank if greenhouse is shut down for any length of time. Be sure drain connection will accommodate hose, drain line as shown in picture, or whatever drain system you plan to install.

C. Connector near top of tank to accommodate 4-inch plastic overflow pipe.

D. If more than one tank is used, a connector is required near bottom of each tank to accommodate 4-inch plastic connecting pipe. *Caution:* If toddlers are going to be around, install lid with a hasp on each tank. This way tank(s) can be kept under lock and key. Small children could be drowned if they climbed into a tank with water in it.

Locate tank in ground with approximately 1½ feet above grade so it is convenient to dip water with a bucket or sprinkling can. To aid in preventing tank from rusting, dig a pit which, when lined with concrete blocks (see section on how to lay concrete blocks in Chapter IV), will be slightly wider and longer than tank. Allow for about 4 inches of sand, on which are placed 4-inch concrete blocks (not mortared together) face down to form a base for supporting tank and to drain seep water. As an additional rust-preventive measure, coat outside of tank below grade, including bottom, with aluminum mastic, which the tinner can supply.

When aluminum mastic is fairly dry, connect hose or plastic drain pipes to connector(s) B and lower tank(s) in prepared hole(s). Place a shut-off valve at a convenient location in drain line before connecting it to sanitary sewer or sump. (Note: See Chapter V for making joints waterproof with cement for the plastic pipe used in your system.)

Next connect one end of 4-inch plastic overflow pipe to connector C. Continue adding pipe to sanitary sewer or to an area lower than the greenhouse floor. If you have more than one tank, connect them with 4-inch plastic pipe cemented to connectors D.

Now bring downspout E from gutter through greenhouse wall to top of tank where downspout fits inside elbow F. To prevent connection from becoming loose, drill a small hole, top side, to accommodate a metal screw. Along the way from gutter to top of tank, use a pipe strap every four to six feet to hold downspout firmly in place to some solid object. If elbow F does not rest firmly in place on top of tank edge, hold in place with a pipe strap held to tank with two metal screws.

## WATERING DEVICES

Watering devices vary from the simple watering can to sophisticated, automatic watering systems.

### Basic Equipment

1. Hose or hoses equipped with nozzles.
2. Watering can.
3. Water breaker (metal device) fastened to end of hose to reduce force of stream.
4. Hand-operated mister or fogger if system is not automatic.
5. Plant markers; these indicate amount of watering.

**Watering Tray**

*IX-2*

**IX-2.**    This is a simple and inexpensive way to water valuable potted plants when you are busy or just "want to get away from it all for a few days." The illustration is of tray cut to show its make-up. The 2- x 6-foot wood frame, or size to suit, is made from pieces of 1 x 4-inch lumber. Place boards on edge, using 3 8-penny coated nails at each corner to fasten frame together. To keep from splitting face of boards, drill holes slightly smaller than nail shank at nail locations.

Cut a piece of black 4 mil polyethylene about 10 inches larger than tray area. Then drape the polyethylene over tray, pressing down to bottom and into corners, forming a lining. Using a staple gun with ½-inch staples, spaced about 2 inches apart, fasten polyethylene to outside of tray. Since the tray has no solid bottom, position it on bench, shelf, or floor. Fill tray to about one inch from top with vermiculite. Place potted plants on top of vermiculite and almost fill tray with water. During your absence, plants absorb needed moisture by capillary attraction. It's a good idea to make a trial run to determine exactly how long you can depend on the system between waterings. Usually, it is between two and three weeks.

**Automatic Watering Systems**

Automatic watering systems are ideal for applying water and liquid fertilizer economically and uniformly. It only takes about ten minutes to water an entire bench, since the water is applied at a rate of about $\frac{1}{10}$ gallon per minute per foot of pipe. Systems can be purchased to accommodate almost any bench size. Generally, they can be installed with such simple tools as a knife, screwdriver, ice pick, and nozzle wrench. One person can handle the work, which is usually 4 hours for each 100 feet of bench.

## CARBON DIOXIDE GENERATOR

**IX-3.**    Additional carbon dioxide ($CO_2$) added to the greenhouse atmosphere produces better plant growth. This is particularly important where potted flowers are grown. For an effective job, all you need is a carbon dioxide generator, as shown in the picture, a supply of electricity, and either natural or LP gas. The unit is simple to install. There is no wasted space, since it hangs from rafters and does not have ductwork.

*IX-3*

## SHADING CLOTH

**IX-4.**    The picture shows a simple frame built over the bench. When it's time for these flowers to go to bed, the gardener pulls the shading cloth over the sides and top of frame, creating a night effect.

## CUBIC FOOT MEASURING BOX

**IX-5.**    If your operation is medium-to-large, a cubic foot measuring box comes in handy. Since 12-inch lumber is actually 11½ inches wide, the following dimensions will give you a box within a few inches of holding an exact cubic foot of material. Saw two pieces 13 inches long and a second pair 14 inches long. Then position boards

*IX-4*

on edge, lapping them together to nail through face near end of one board into end grain of adjoining board. Use 8-penny coated nails, first drilling holes in face boards slightly smaller than nail shank. Cut bottom boards to fit inside. Then fasten in place with 8-penny coated nails, first drilling holes in face boards as described above. Three pieces of scrap waterpipe and two bolts and nuts make a solid handle for each side, as

*IX-5*

shown in the picture. (Note: If you have trouble with sides pulling apart, you can lick it once and for all by using metal corner braces as illustrated in Chapter III, Figure 11c.)

## BENCH

*IX-6*

**IX-6.** The picture shows a substantial bench, which is quickly put together. Place 8 x 16-inch concrete blocks as shown. Use 1¼-inch pipe as stringers. So long as it is heavy pipe and not rusted through, it can be either new or used. Cut to length with hacksaw. Then position on tops of blocks as shown. Make the tray 32 inches wide x 8 feet long or dimensions to suit requirements. You can use 6-inch boards, preferably redwood, spaced ⅛ inch apart and nailed to 2 x 4 stringers spaced 3 feet apart for the bottom, and 6-inch boards for the sides—or a piece of corrugated asbestos for the bottom and ⅜ x 6-inch flat asbestos sheets for the sides. Asbestos material is carried by most lumberyards. It can be cut to size with a masonry saw. Use flat, metal corner braces, as shown in Chapter III, Figure 11c, and bolts and nuts to fasten side and end pieces to bottom piece.

## GARAGE DOOR

**IX-7.** With labor costs spiraling year after year, labor-saving devices are fast becoming more and more the rule rather than the exception with

*IX-7*

many greenhouse gardeners. If you are planning a medium-to-large operation requiring the use of a truck, one device to consider is an overhead garage door. The door can be installed as part of the greenhouse wall, so that supplies can be brought in and produce moved out with the least amount of wasted energy. Or a garage can be built adjoining the greenhouse, as shown in the picture, thus losing none of the plant area to roadway. Garage doors can be purchased from lumberyards and mail-order firms. Be sure the door is of the right height and width to suit your needs. Door packages include the door, adjustable extension springs, hinges, steel headtrack, lock with two keys, outside handle, hardware, and installation instructions.

# II

# Greenhouse Construction

# X

# Mini-Greenhouse Models

## HOTBED OR COLD FRAME

A hotbed or cold frame is actually one and the same thing, either can be constructed in the same way. Their differences lie in method of heating and seasonal usage. Manure, electric light bulbs, warm air from an open basement window or heating cable, in addition to heat from the sun, are means of heating hotbeds, while the sun only provides heat for a cold frame. Both require a southern exposure, free of shade. Generally, hotbeds are used to start plants early. Then, as the regular planting season approaches, a cold frame is used to start plants. Some gardeners start plants in a hotbed, transferring them later to field or cold frame.

### Permanent Hotbed Model

**X-1.** The permanent hotbed model illustrated here is heated with an electric heating cable. Be-

cause of the even, accurate control of bed temperature, it is possible to raise uniform, quality plants. Actually, if this type of hotbed is properly constructed and electricity is available at a realistic cost, it may be cheaper to operate than other kinds of heating devices. This is particularly so if you live in an "all electric home" where a special electricity rate has already been established. When estimating any kind of operational cost, time of year, weather conditions, type of construction, management, location, and electric rate per kilowatt hour are important factors. As a general rule, a 3 x 6-foot hotbed uses 30-60 kilowatt hours of electricity per month.

X-2

**X-2.** In addition to a shovel, hammer, carpenter's plane, hand saw, paint brush, and tools used in Chapter VI for making electrical installations, you will need a drill, drill bit, and a caulking gun. See glossary for definition and/or use.

1. Drill and drill bit to suit requirements.
2. Caulking gun designed to accept caulking cartridges.

X-1

The following table lists material required for making an electrically heated hotbed 3 x 6 feet. If a hotbed of different dimensions is required, adjust dimensions accordingly.

### Materials for Hotbed

| Names or parts | Description |
| --- | --- |
| Form lumber* | 2 pieces 2 x 6 x 10 feet |
| Form lumber* | 1 piece 2 x 6 x 12 feet |
| Corner stakes | 1 x 2s or scrap lumber; length to suit |
| Form stakes* | 1 x 2s or scrap lumber; length to suit |
| Concrete** | Proportion of 1 cement: 2 sand: 3 rock |
| Sides and rear frame members A and B | 1 piece 2 x 12 x 16 feet |
| Front frame member C | 1 piece 2 x 8 x 3 feet |
| Nails | Approx. ½ lb. 16-penny |
| Nails | Approx. 2 ozs. 8-penny |
| Nails | Approx. 1 oz. 6-penny |
| Weather stripping board D | 1 piece 1 x 4 inch x 16 feet |
| Sash supports E (optional) | See text |
| Greenhouse sash F | 3 x 6 feet |
| Hinges G | Two 1½ - x 2-inches fast-pin rust-resistant butt hinges and screws |
| Prop stick H | Assembly consisting of ½ x 2 x 16-inch plywood, ¼ x 2½-inch carriage bolt, washer, and wing nut to fit |
| Caulking | Tube of latex caulking |
| Heating cable 1 | Either 115 volts or 230 volts |
| Sand 2 | Area of bed by 2 inches thick |
| Hardware cloth 4 | Same as bed area with ½-inch mesh |
| Electric outlet box | Standard size |
| Electric outlet | Standard size |
| Thermostat 5 | "Open" and "close" range not more than 5° with operating range between 30°-120° |
| Copper Napthenate | 2 percent |
| Paint | Color of your choice |
| Paint brush | Size to suit |

\* Not required if concrete blocks are used.
\*\* If concrete blocks are not used, use only enough concrete to pour a 6-inch wide footing.

## Location

Successful operation of a hotbed requires a good location as a prerequisite to actual construction. Consider these points in selecting a site:

1.  Determine size of hotbed to meet your requirements.
2.  Be sure good, natural drainage is available, so excess moisture does not collect beneath the bed. If necessary, prepare bed for artificial drainage—as described later.
3.  Have bed level, even if it requires fill to make it so.
4.  Locate bed near as possible to water and electrical supplies.
5.  Be sure bed is clear of shade and shadows.
6.  Locate so windbreak slows prevailing winds. (Windbreaks are described in Chapter IV.)

## Construction

X-3

**X-3.** Although side walls of beds can be constructed entirely of wood, it is better to build them on either a concrete or concrete block foundation resting on a concrete footing when electricity is used for heating. For a substantial base for a hotbed or cold frame see suggestions for building footings and foundations in Chapter IV. The picture shows a 3 x 6-foot poured concrete foundation with forms removed. Forms were made of 2 x 6s cut to proper dimensions, nailed at the corners with 16-penny nails, and held in place with 1 x 2 wood stakes.

If it is necessary to place cinders or gravel under bed for proper drainage, excavate area inside foundation to a depth of 8 inches. Now fill excavation to a depth of 6 inches with either cinders or gravel, tapping solid. Place a light covering such as burlap over the fill, so that water will pass through but sand will not. Follow with a 2-inch bed of sand. *Caution:* The sand acts as a protector for the heating cable when it is installed later. The chemical reaction between cinders and cable covering or sharp pieces of gravel may cause havoc by shorting out the cable.

X-5

X-4

**X-4.** Use 2 x 12s for back or north wall A and side walls B, and a 2 x 8 for front wall C. Cut wall material to length; when fastened together outside faces will form a continuous wall extending above concrete foundation, as illustrated. Next bevel top edges of back piece A and front piece C so their top edges will be on the same plane when assembled. Saw side pieces B with a slope, so top edges of the four pieces will be on the same plane when assembled. Picture shows how the four pieces form the walls and are fastened together with 16-penny nails. (Note: You can economize if you spend time reworking the used lumber to fit your hotbed specifications.)

**X-5.** Cut three 1 x 4-inch boards D to fit around top and side edges of hotbed frame as shown in the picture. These boards serve as weather stripping. Next fasten boards D to frame, using 8-penny nails spaced about 14 inches apart. Be sure weather-stripping boards extend 5/4 inch above top of hotbed frame (same distance as thickness of sash frame). Since sash should extend slightly over edge of front wall to shed water,

a weather-stripping board is not required here. For better insulation, bank some of the soil removed from the excavation against outside of the concrete foundation. Do not bring soil in contact with wood side walls. Further weatherproof by caulking inside and outside crack between top of foundation and side walls.

X-6

**X-6.** If your hotbed is the width of two or more sashes, use appropriate number of removable sash supports E between sashes not adjoining the walls. Make them as shown by fastening center of a 1 x 4-inch board to a 1 x 2-inch board with 6-penny nails spaced approximately 14 inches apart. It serves as a sash support and also provides good weather stripping. (Note: 1 x 4-inch board is cut to fit loosely between front and rear frame members, while 1 x 2-inch board is cut to fit flush with outside of front and rear frame members.)

**X-7.** Position sash F onto top edges of side walls and front frame. Use two 1½ x 2-inch rust-resistant butt hinges G and accompanying screws to fasten sash to rear weather-stripping board.

X-7

Plane sash edges if they bind against weather-stripping boards.

**X-8.** Either use a prop stick assembly like the one in the following greenhouse model or like H, as illustrated. Make it from a ½-inch piece of weatherproof plywood. Shape the wood ½ x 2 x 16 inches long, as shown. Next saw notches to support sash in open position, follow by boring a ¼-inch hole through middle of face about 2 inches from end, opposite notches. Now bore a ¼-inch hole near end of one of the side walls. From outside, drive in a ¼ x 2½-inch carriage bolt. Using hole, slip prop stick (notches toward rear wall) over carriage bolt, followed with a washer and wing nut.

Paint entire frame and sash frame with 2 percent copper napthenate solution to retard decay. When perfectly dry follow up with two coats of exterior paint. See Chapter III for information on painting.

X-8

### Heating Cable

If you plan to heat your hotbed with an electric heating cable, see information on code requirements and wiring installations in Chapter VI.

The right kind of heating cable for your size greenhouse can be obtained from most greenhouse supply houses. Cables are either lead- or plastic-covered. Both provide satisfactory service. Before purchasing a cable, find out how many watts per square foot of bed area are required for your locality. Generally, the range is between 10 watts per square foot in southern areas to 16 watts per square foot in northern areas. This information can be obtained by writing to the nearest greenhouse supplier or the State Extension Agriculture Engineer, who is usually located on campus at the state university.

Cables vary both as to watts per foot and to length. Also, they may be purchased for either 115-volt or 230-volt circuits. 115-volt cables are satisfactory for small beds, 4-sash size or less. For larger beds, 230-volt cables are recommended.

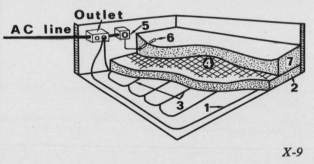

X-9

**X-9.** If drainage is poor, prepare bottom of bed with cinders or gravel, burlap, and sand as previously recommended. If drainage is good, position electric cable 1 on bed floor to be covered by two inches of sand 2. As you place cable, be sure loops 3 are spaced correctly.

Correct spacing between loops 3 or sections of cable and outside cable and walls, which is half the spacing distance between cables, is estimated as follows:

Spacing between loops (in inches) =
$$\frac{12 \times \text{watts per foot of cable}}{\text{Wattage required per square foot of hotbed}}$$

Sample problem: 60-foot cable rated at 400 watts with 10 watts per square foot required for bed.

Spacing between loops =

$$\frac{12 \times (400 \div 60)}{10} = \frac{12 \times 6.7}{10} = \frac{80.4}{10}$$

= 8 inch spacing between loops.
½ of 8 inches = 4 inch spacing between outside cable and walls.

Heed these five precautions when laying the cable:

1. Heating cable connections must be tight as well as waterproof.
2. From time of unpacking, never allow cable to kink. To do so may create a break, causing a short. This is particularly true with lead-covered cable.
3. Never place metal, even hardware cloth, in direct contact with installed cable.
4. Never shorten cable length. Cable may overheat and burn out.
5. Do not crisscross one cable or section of cable over another.

With two inches of sand 2 covering cable, follow with a ½-inch mesh hardware (metal) cloth 4 covering to help prevent cable damage when working top soil with sharp tools.

Purchase a thermostat 5 meeting these three specifications:

1. An "open" and "close" range of not more than 5°.
2. A remote-temperature bulb 6 to be buried in the top soil 7.
3. An operating range between 30°-120° F.

Connect thermostat 5 in the circuit as shown above. If different temperatures for different sections of a large bed are desired, install sufficient thermostats to govern desired range.

For satisfactory operation, position remote-temperature bulb 6 a third of the way across width of bed and an equal distance from end wall following placement of four to six inches of top soil 7 over hardware cloth 4. Bury temperature bulb 6 approximately one inch in top soil 7, being sure bulb 6 is located between heating cable 1. Otherwise, you will obtain a false reading.

## PLANT GROWTH

Here are six helpful hints regarding plant growth in electrically heated hotbeds:

1. Do not seed bed too early in the season—plants grow rapidly.
2. Use two thermometers to maintain proper soil and air temperatures: one for checking soil temperature, the other for checking air temperature above plant height. Be sure soil thermometer is at same depth in the soil as the remote-thermostat bulb.
3. Most seeds require a planting temperature of between 70°-75° F.
4. Following germination of seeds, hold temperatures to suit type of plant. For example, lettuce, cabbage, and cauliflower are cool season crops that need a daytime temperature of 60°-65° F. On the other hand, tomatoes, peppers, melons, and eggplant are warm season crops that prefer a daytime temperature of 65°-75° F. Maintain night air temperatures of 5°-10° below day air temperatures. Should bed temperature reach 85°, open sash ventilator, but avoid exposing plants to damage from the elements—rain, wind, and extremely low temperatures.
5. Beds heated electrically become dry quickly if not attended properly. Water in early morning so foliage can dry before sunset. Actually, the bed should be moist at all times but never soaking wet.
6. Maintain proper nighttime temperatures by reducing electricity and placing a rug over the bed followed by an equal piece of polyethylene to keep rug dry. Weight with lumber or bricks to keep from blowing off. Remove covering during daylight hours.

## Other Means Of Heating Hotbeds

Although the heating cable is considered by many to be the most desirable way to heat a hotbed, others do a fine job of germinating and raising plants in hotbeds heated in one of several other ways.

### Manure

One of the old-time ways of heating a hotbed is through the use of manure. Here the excavation is filled with manure, followed by the placement of 4 inches of top soil. *Caution:* For reasons of health do not use human feces.

*Incandescent Light Bulbs*

Sometimes small beds are heated by the warmth from several incandescent light bulbs, connected in series to a 115-volt circuit. For wiring details, see Chapter VI.

Several small bulbs are preferable to a single large bulb. For instance, suppose a 200-watt bulb supplies ample heat to a bed during the coldest winter day. During an average winter day, the choice is no heat or turning on the bulb and ventilating, thereby wasting electricity in heating the outside air. When four 50-watt bulbs, connected in series, are lighted, heat for the coldest day is provided. On warmer days, simply turn off one or more bulbs until the correct temperature is reached.

*Basement Furnace*

By building a hotbed adjacent to a basement window, you can make use of furnace heat. With window raised, hotbed is heated from basement air.

This hotbed can be built in the same way as the permanent hotbed model described above with one exception—eliminate the rear end wall and its corresponding foundation and footing. Be sure rear frame member of hotbed is high enough so top end of sash fits against foundation above top of window.

**Window Greenhouse Model**

**X-10.** This window greenhouse can be installed without mutilating the window frame, because the model is constructed to fit the opening as it rests upon the window sill. Four wood screws hold it securely in place and require only a few minutes to install. Incidentally, if window greenhouse is removed sometime in the future, fill each screwhole with glazing compound, followed with a dab of paint, and the window frame looks as good as new. Manufactured window greenhouses similar to this can be bought, but you can make your own and save 50-60 percent!

In case you wonder what good a window greenhouse is, here are a few uses:

1.  Seedlings and plants can be started in late winter for early-bird planting outdoors as soon as weather conditions permit.

X-10

2.  Orchids can be grown.
3.  Tender outdoor plants can be held over from one season to the next.
4.  An amazing number of house plants can be placed in it during the entire year.
5.  Last but not least, you, too, can have your own greenhouse even if you live several stories above the ground in an apartment building. Before starting the project, however, clear it with the building owner or superintendent and the zoning regulations.

A cat sitting on the window sill inside serves as a "watch dog." When she slowly twists her head back and forth, seemingly gazing off into space, I know a fly or other insect(s) has invaded the greenhouse.

The arborvitae evergreen and the flowers in the greenhouse have the effect of bringing the outdoors right into the house.

Tools required are a hand saw, hammer, screwdriver, nail set, and the use of a power saw. See glossary for definition and/or use.

The following table lists materials for building a window greenhouse where the inside measurements of the window frame are 36 inches wide and 55 inches high. For different dimensions, alter the list accordingly. With the exception of the bottom board, widths and thicknesses of lumber listed should remain the same.

### Window Greenhouse Materials

| Names or parts | Description |
| --- | --- |
| Frame members A, B, C, D, and F | 4 pieces 1 x 2 x 12 feet |
| Frame members E and H | 1 piece 1 x 2 x 14 feet |
| Bottom board G | 1 piece 1 x 12 x 3 feet |
| Hinges I | 1½ x 2-inch fast-pin, rust-resistant butt |
| Assembly J | 1 carriage bolt ¼ x 3 inches with washer and wing nut, ¾ x 4-inches fast-pin, rust-resistant strap hinge, and 1 piece weatherproof plywood ½ x 2 x 16 inches |
| Shelves K | Plate glass, number and size depending upon requirements |
| Glass for frame members | Double-strength, pieces for two sides and front frames, sizes to suit requirements |
| Angle irons L | ⅝ x 2 inch with screws |
| Nails | Approx. ⅜ lbs. 6-penny finish |
| Nails | Approx. 1 oz. 4-penny finish |
| Glue | Waterproof, amount to suit requirements |
| Glazing compound | Amount to suit requirements |
| Glazing points | Number to suit requirements |
| Wood preservative (optional) | 2 percent napthenate |
| Paint (optional if redwood is used) | Amount and color to suit requirements |
| Caulking | Tube of latex caulking compound |

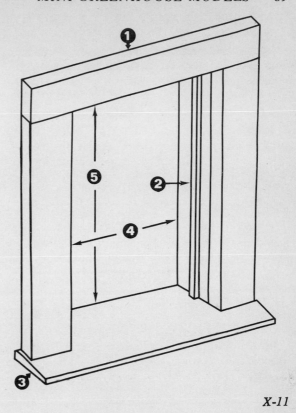

*X-11*

**X-11.** Select a window that will catch a lot of sun in cold weather. Remember, too, you can always grow plants by giving them fluorescent light if your home is in the shade (see Chapter VI). For use later, become familiar with window frame parts. The illustration shows only those parts of the window frame involved in building a window greenhouse. Window casing 1, window stop 2, and window sill 3. Measure and record your window width 4 and height 5. (Note: In the illustration, measurements were 36 inches wide and 55 inches high. Perhaps your window is of different dimensions. If so, change the material list accordingly.) If your window frame does not have a storm window, measurements will be greenhouse outside dimensions, because it will be positioned inside window frame against window stop. 2. If your window frame has a storm window, measurements will be greenhouse inside measurements, because it will be positioned onto outside window casing. Since window sill 3 slopes, be certain measurement 5 is taken parallel to one of the window casings 1.

### Assembling

**X-12.** If carpentry work is not exactly your bag, see the section titled Woodworking Suggestions in Chapter III before beginning actual construction. Be sure lengths and widths of assembled parts fit *your* window frame dimensions. Although the greenhouse illustrated here has a depth of 12 inches, you may want more room. In this case, up to 18 inches is a practical depth.

X-12

Before starting construction, examine the picture showing how your side frame pieces will fit together to form one of two side frames A.

X-13

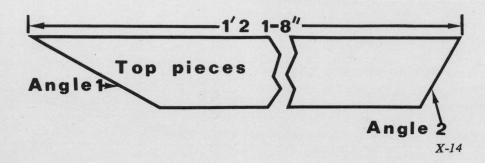

X-14

**X-13.**  Now begin the construction of the two greenhouse side frames A. (Note: I used redwood for the entire framework, because it is not affected by rot or vermin. It is easy to work and the finished product blends with most architecture.) Select enough 1 x 2s to make the two side frames A, consisting of top, side, and bottom pieces. Then, using a set of dado blades on a power saw, or making two cuts with a regular circle saw blade, cut a rabbet (¼ inch wide x ⅜ inch deep)—shown by arrow—along face edge that will hold glass in place later.

**X-14.**  Use the half-scale angles in the picture as a guide for cutting top angles of front and rear corner frames to size. Cut tops of rear corner frames to angle 1. You can use the angles by placing a T-bevel over angles, one at time, positioning and locking blade in place, transferring T-bevel to top edge of 1 x 2, marking angle, than sawing. You can also obtain the angles by tracing them on cardboard, transferring same to the 1 x 2s. When you cut the angles, be sure shortest distance between them adjoins the rabbet

cut. A crooked window could result in one window frame height being different from the other. Check the exact height of both rear corner pieces; then saw 45° cuts on bottom end of each piece. Next measure and saw 45° cuts on bottom ends of front corner pieces. Check on two things: 1. Both front and rear frame cuts should be on the same plane later when assembled; and 2. length of the two rear corner pieces are window height less ¾ inch (thickness of movable top frame). Rabbet the two front corner frames used later for glazing front glass. Be sure rabbet on each piece is on a diagonal from rabbet made previously for side glass.

Decide on depth of greenhouse. Then cut side, bottom pieces at a 45° angle. Shortest distance between angle cuts adjoin rabbet cut. Referring to half-size top piece in illustration above, mark and saw side, top pieces. Angle 1 fits top ends of rear corner frames; angle 2 fits top ends of front corner frames. In the event that you decide on a depth greater than 12 inches, simply cut side, top, and bottom pieces to your requirements. The angles need not change; only the pieces are longer.

X-15

X-16

**X-15.** Now that four pieces are cut for making each side frame, brush waterproof glue on each of the angle cuts. The picture shows how to fasten the corners together with two finish nails, a 4-penny near the corner and a 6-penny approximately 1¼ inches from the corner. If nails split the wood, predrill a hole, slightly smaller in diameter than the nails, through top pieces of wood. Countersink the nails. (Note: Follow instructions exactly on the container for the waterproof glue.) When the two side frames are completed, compare them with Fig. 12 as well as checking them against window frame opening. Make similar checks from time to time with the window frame opening as you complete remainder of frame assembly.

**X-16.** Decide now on shelf height as well as number of shelves you want. Then cut required number of shelf brackets B from 1 x 2 stock, making them as long as side frame width minus 1¾ inches (width of rabbet cut plus thickness of front and rear shelf brackets F to be installed later). Using waterproof glue and two 4-penny finish nails near each end, fasten shelf brackets B to inside of side frames, being sure rabbet cut on front edge is clear. Countersink the nails.

**X-17.** Cut two bottom, cross pieces C from 1 x 2-inch stock as long as sides are wide less 1½ inches (thickness of front and rear bottom frame members shown in the step to follow). Using waterproof glue, position bottom face of cross piece C, centered and flush, with bottom edge of lower side frame A. Fasten in place by driving three 6-penny finish nails through side frame A into edge of cross member C. When both cross pieces are in place, countersink nails.

X-17

X-18

**X-18.** Using 1 x 2-inch stock, cut front and rear bottom frame members D width of window opening minus 1½ inches (thickness of the two side frames.) Now rabbet front bottom piece only. With two 6-penny nails and waterproof glue, at each end fasten front and rear bottom pieces D flush to bottom edge of side frames.

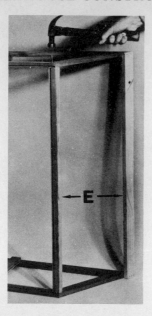

X-19

**X-19.** Next cut and assemble front and rear top frame members E from 1 x 2-inch stock. Begin by cutting front top frame member E same length as bottom frame members D in preceding step. Then bevel top edge until it is flush with top edges of side frames. Next cut rabbet along lower outside edge. Position and fasten in place with waterproof glue and two 6-penny finish nails at each end.

Cut rear top frame member length of window width or same length as front top frame plus 1½ inches, since it is to be fastened on top of side frames. Bevel one edge so it will fit flush with their rear edges. Fasten rear top frame member E onto top edge of side frames with waterproof glue and two 6-penny finish nails at each end.

**X-20.** From 1 x 2s, cut front and rear shelf

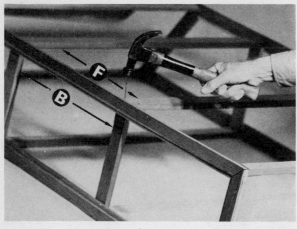

X-20

brackets F to fit between side frames and against and flush with end shelf brackets B. Fasten in place with 6-penny finish nails and waterproof glue.

X-21

**X-21.** Cut bottom board G from 1 x 12-inch stock to fit inside the four bottom frame members and rest on top of cross member C. Fasten in place by driving 6-penny finish nails—spaced about 8 inches apart—through bottom frame members into edges of bottom board G. (Note: If bottom board in your greenhouse is wider than a 1-foot board, use ¾-inch weatherproof plywood.)

X-22

**X-22.** Rabbet enough 1 x 2-inch stock for making top movable frame H, which is to fit against top rear frame member E and flush with remaining top frame members. Using 45° angle cuts, saw stock and assemble similarly to previously assembled side frames. I do not recommend beveling front edge of top frame H. Run off of rain water is better without beveling. Fasten top frame H to rear frame member E with two 1½ x 2-inch fast-pin, rust-resistant butt hinges I and accompanying flat-head screws.

*X-23*

**X-23.** The picture shows a ¾ x 4-inch fast-pin, rust-resistant strap hinge screwed to bottom face of top side of movable frame member H, approximately 1 inch from face of front top frame member E and to a ½ x 2 x 12-inch piece of weatherproof, plywood prop stick J, with 5⁄16-inch holes spaced approximately 1½ inches apart, which holds movable top frame in desired open position with aid of ¼ x 3-inch carriage bolt (shown by arrow) fastened through front top frame member E. Movable top frame is held in desired open position by placing the carriage bolt through selected hole in prop stick J followed by a washer and a wing nut tightened in place.

### Finishing

Check nails; all should be countersunk. If the greenhouse is made from redwood, give it two coats of redwood preservative to retain its natural beauty. Redwood, like other kinds of wood, can be given two coats of quality exterior paint, color of your choice, if you wish. For further painting suggestions, see Chapter III.

### Installing The Glass

Accurately measure width and length of rabbeted areas of each of the four frames requiring glass. Then order double-strength glass ⅛ inch less in width and length for each frame. Using glazier's points, glaze as explained in Chapter III.

Order plate glass shelves K, as shown in the following step, width to suit requirements and lengths with edges flush with outside edge of end shelf brackets. This allows for ¾-inch air space at each end of shelf for air circulation during ventilation periods.

*X-24*

**X-24.** If you checked assembled parts of the greenhouse against window opening during construction, you should encounter no problem with the installation. Using flat-head wood screws, fasten angle iron L on each side frame near top and bottom. Then position greenhouse to window opening, fastening angle irons with screws securely to window frame. If angle irons require shortening, use a hacksaw. For a weatherproof job, use caulking gun to caulk sides, top, and bottom edges where they come in contact with window casing.

If your window greenhouse is not protected from rain with a suitable roof soffit, fashion and apply a strip of plastic as a hinge strip on top of ventilating frame and next to top window casing. See following chapter, Figure 14, for making one.

# XI

# Quonset Economy Model

**XI-1.** This Quonset economy greenhouse is truly a welcome addition to any home. The structure lends itself readily to the work of the year round hobbyist, who wants to grow different species of flowers, ornamental plants, start plants for an outdoor garden, and provide fresh vegetables and herbs for the table, thereby putting a dent in the food budget.

This model, with its curved arch design, lets in a fantastic amount of light, so important for year round gardening. Furthermore, it is easy to build,

relatively inexpensive, of sturdy construction, and laid out in simple modules. The latter makes it easy to expand or contract simply by adding or subtracting pipe bows. Lengths can vary anywhere between 12 feet and 100 feet without a single construction technique being changed. Widths can range from 10-30 feet simply by the use of thicker and longer pipe bows. Also, with minor changes in the design a portable model 10 x 12½ feet can be quickly, easily constructed.

*XI-1*

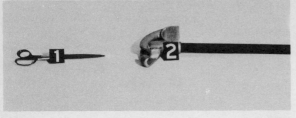

XI-2

**XI-2.** You will need a piece of chalk, carpenter's hammer, ball of cord, plumb bob, carpenter's level, pliers, paint brush and those tools illustrated to build this greenhouse. See glossary for definition and/or use of each.

1. Large pair of scissors
2. Pipe bender

The following table lists materials for building a 10 x 20-foot Quonset greenhouse. It is designed in modules 2½ feet long. If you need a longer or shorter size, add or subtract pipe bows (spaced 2 feet 6 inches apart) until your personal requirements are met. Adjust other materials accordingly. (Note: Changes in material requirements necessary for increasing widths wider than 10 feet are given, in the appropriate steps, as well as those necessary for a portable greenhouse 10 feet x 12 feet 6 inches.) If you wish to alter the basic model dimensions given here, I suggest you begin by reading the complete chapter and change material requirements on the following list as you read:

**Quonset Greenhouse**

| Parts | Description |
|---|---|
| Piece of chalk | Chalkboard chalk |
| Iron stakes A | 2 pieces ¾-inch x 21 feet galvanized water pipes |
| Pipe bows B and ridge pipe C | 10 pieces ½-inch x 21-feet galvanized water pipes |
| U bolts | 9, size to fit ½-inch pipe |
| Gable framing | |
|    Front plate D | 1 piece 2 x 4 10 feet |
|    Studs front and rear E, F, and G | 9 pieces 2 x 4s 8 feet |
|    Cross members H and I | 2 pieces 2 x 4s 10 feet |
|    Top plate J | 2 pieces 1 x 4s 16 feet |
| Pipe clamps K | 12 pieces ½-inch galvanized |
| Pipe clamps for fastening pipe stakes to baseboards | 18 pieces ¾-inch galvanized |

| Parts | Description |
|---|---|
| Baseboard L | 2 pieces 2 x 8s x 20 feet 1 piece 2 x 8 x 18 feet |
| Finish | Redwood preservative for redwood or 2 percent copper naphthenate and paint for other wood in amounts to suit |
| Covering | |
| Wire mesh M | 70 feet of 4 x 4-inch x 12-gauge galvanized welded wire mesh 72 inches wide |
| Wire ties | 25 feet of galvanized wire #14 gauge |
| Polyethylene N and O | 35 feet of 6 mil clear 20 feet wide |
| Laths or scrap lumber | 210 lineal feet 1½ x ¼ inch |
| Polypropylene tape (optional) P | Sold 1½-inches x 300-foot rolls |
| Ideal clips (optional) | 72—¾ or 1 inch depending upon pipe size used |
| Nails | Approx. 1¾ lbs. 16-penny box |
| Nails | Approx. ¼ lb. 8-penny box |
| Nails | Approx. 3 oz. 6-penny box |
| Nails | Approx. ¾ lb 4-penny box |
| Door Q, hinges, and lock to suit | |

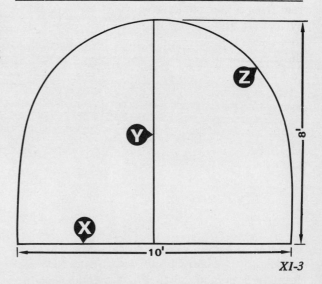

XI-3

**XI-3.** Begin by marking a layout arc used to govern shape of bows during pipe bending process. Use a piece of chalk to mark base line 10 feet long on a flat surface, such as a driveway or garage floor. Then mark 8-foot perpendicular line Y beginning at midpoint of base line to locate high point of pipe bow line. Now connect end points of base line X by marking curved line Z through top point of perpendicular line Y. (Note: Bow line is not a perfect semicircle, although you can make it so if you desire. By so doing you reduce the height, giving more width. If you do decide on making this dimensional change, you may find a lack of head room an inconvenience later on.)

## Construction

*XI-4*

**XI-4.** Using a pipe bender, which you can rent from a tool rental company, form pipe bows by making gradual bends on the 9½-inch x 21-foot galvanized water pipes until they conform to the pipe bow line laid out previously.

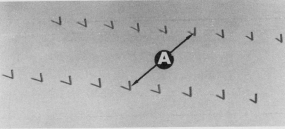

*XI-5*

**XI-5.** Layout exact length and width of greenhouse on chosen site with nylon cord and four wood corner stakes. For a permanent structure, prepare footing, foundation, and wall. For layout details, see Chapter IV.

If you do not have access to a pipe cutter, use a hacksaw to cut 18 iron stakes A 2 feet 4 inches long from two pieces of ¾-inch galvanized water pipe 21 feet long.

Drive pipe A 19 inches into the ground at each

of the four corners with a hammer. Align tops of stakes level with each other with a line level and cord. Then drive inbetween stakes A into the ground at intervals of 2½ feet on both long sides of the layout. Now check with a stretched line between corner stakes to be sure tops of stakes are level with corner stakes. (Note: For a greenhouse longer or shorter than 20 feet, be sure correct number of stakes are properly placed to meet your requirements.

If you build a foundation (described in Chapter IV), you can set stakes A in concrete for a poured foundation, or grout them in the block voids if you build a concrete block foundation. *Caution:* To increase the width of the greenhouse, use ¾-inch galvanized water pipes for the bows and 1-inch galvanized water pipes for the stakes for widths between 15-20 feet. For widths between 22-30 feet, use 1-inch galvanized water pipes for the bows and 1½-inch galvanized water pipes for the stakes. Pipe connectors can be used to increase 21-foot pipe to required length.

(Portable Greenhouse Note: To build a portable greenhouse 10 x 12½ feet, use ½-inch galvanized water pipes for the bows, lengths to suit.) Some builders construct their arc (Step 3) so perpendicular line Y is only 4½ feet high. The purpose here is to construct a portable greenhouse just high enough to allow the gardener to work comfortably in a sitting position. With ½-inch pipes for the bows, use ¾-inch galvanized pipes for the stakes. Neither drive them into the ground nor use grout or concrete. Skip the following step.

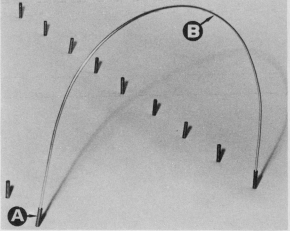

*XI-6*

**XI-6.** Mix some concrete grout as described in Chapter III. Then fill each of the stakes A within 3 inches of their tops. Let the concrete stand for 24 hours, then position ends of pipe bows B into pipe stakes A.

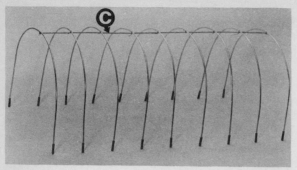

XI-7

**XI-7.** Cut 20-foot ridge pipe C from a 21-foot length of ½-inch galvanized water pipe. Then position underneath side of pipe bows. Use 9 U bolts designed for ½-inch pipe to fasten it securely to pipe bows, being sure spacing is maintained at 2½ feet. Short pieces of galvanized wire twisted around ridge pipe and pipe bows is another way to make the fastenings. (Note: Any time pieces of wire are used, be sure to make bends out of the way so protruding ends will not puncture greenhouse covering later or become a hazard to personnel.)

*Caution:* For greenhouse widths between 15-30 feet, use ¾-inch galvanized water pipe for ridge pipe C. For widths between 22-30 feet, add two purlins to the pipe framework. Make these from ¾-inch galvanized water pipes, each located parallel to and five feet on each side of ridge pipe C. Both positioning and fastening purlins are done in exactly the same way as ridge pipe C.

For ridges and purlins longer than 20 feet, connect sections of pipe together with pipe connectors.

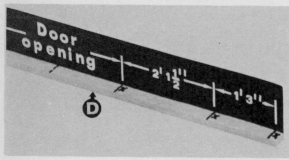

XI-8

**XI-8.** Frame gable ends next, beginning with the one in front. Use a 10 foot 2 x 4 for bottom board of plate D. Locate center and mark line on plate. Then measure and mark on each side of center line one half of your door opening width. Since I used a 6-foot 8-inch x 3-foot door, ³⁄₁₆ inch was added to 3 feet to allow for door clearance. Next measure distance as shown in picture, and mark lines from door opening toward both ends of plates. Using an X, indicate uprights or studs next to stud marking line as shown. Measurements for left half and right half of plate are the same. (Note: The distance of 2½ feet on each side of door opening provides room for framing in an exhaust fan. If fan is not desired, you can space studs more evenly.)

(Portable Greenhouse Note: 2 x 2 plates and studs—free of knots—are heavy enough for making the portable greenhouse. 2 x 2s can also be used as cross members in the following step, followed by a 1 x 2 top plate in Step 11.

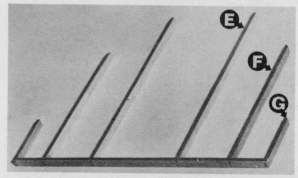

XI-9

**XI-9.** Place plate, markings top side, inbetween and flush with front metal corner stakes. With a plumb bob and string, or a straight edge and a carpenter's level, locate and mark on front pipe bow each stud position. Exact measurements are not indicated here, because each builder will have slight variations in stud length due to personal layout of bow line. For instance, to meet my bow line, studs E, F, and G were 2 feet, 7 feet 8 inches, and 8 feet long respectively. Now cut 2 x 4 studs E and F to length, measuring from top face of bottom plate to bottom of pipe bow less ¾ inch (thickness of top plate to be cut and fastened later). Be sure to cut top ends of these studs at an angle corresponding to bow angle at stud location. Cut 2 x 4 stud G to length, measuring from top face of plate to bottom of pipe bow less 2¼ inch (thickness of top plate plus thickness of cross members). Next mark and cut the three studs on left side in the same manner.

Using two 16-penny box nails, drive two nails through bottom face of plate into end grain of studs.

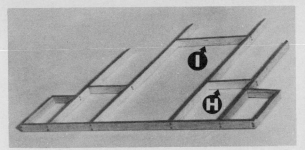

*XI-10*

**XI-10.** Mark and cut four cross members H, getting your measurements between studs where they join plate. Using two 16-penny box nails at each joint, fasten them to studs as shown. Nail one end of outside cross member onto top edge of end studs as indicated. Measure, mark, and cut door opening cross member I, following procedure used in preparing and fastening previous cross members. Position it 6 feet 8¼ inches above plate, then nail in place with four 16-penny box nails.

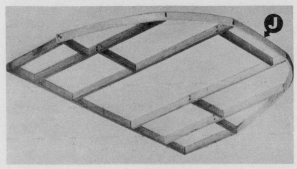

*XI-11*

**XI-11.** Measure, mark, and cut 1 x 4-inch top plate J. My top plate was 16 feet long. If you must make joints in top plate, be sure they are centered directly over top edge of stud. Next position top plate over studs as shown. Fasten with two 8-penny box nails driven through face of top plate into end grain of studs. No need to cut out plate at bottom of door; it can remain to serve as a threshold. (Note: Most 1 x 4s used for top plates will not bend readily, they will break unless they are water-treated first. To do this, unroll plastic covering material. Form a crude trough, in which you place the top plates. Put in enough water so they can soak for 24 hours. Applying top plates soon after the soaking should eliminate the problem of bending and avoid breaking.)

Construct rear gable in the same manner, with one exception: unless a rear door is needed, position and nail cross member I (shown in previous step) approximately four feet above bottom plate.

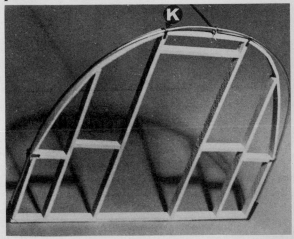

*XI-12*

**XI-12.** A helper is needed to position and fasten gable framework to pipe bows. Place framework in vertical position directly underneath front gable pipe bow. Be sure outside edges of framework are flush with outside edge of gable pipe bow. Next fasten gable pipe bow at its junction with studs. To do this bend ½-inch metal pipe clamp K to fit. Then position it over pipe bow, fastening in place with two 6-penny box nails. For a more secure fastening, use two 10 x 1½-inch round-head wood screws.

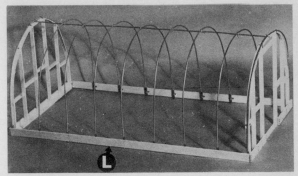

*XI-13*

**XI-13.** Position 2 x 8 x 20-foot baseboards L, one on either side of outside edge of pipe stakes. Next place a ¾-inch pipe clamp over each pipe stake about midway of baseboard. Fasten clamps to baseboards with two 6-penny box nails. For a more secure fastening, substitute 10 x 1½-inch round-head wood screws for the nails. Next, fasten front and rear baseboards L (after cutting to size) to each other at their corners and to the 2 x 4 gable, wood framework. Use three 16-penny box nails for each fastening. Fasten front and rear baseboards L to bottom plate, spacing 16-penny box nails at 16 inch intervals.

(Portable Greenhouse Note: 2 x 4s are plenty large for portable greenhouse baseboards. Since the pipe stakes have no ground or concrete support, use two pipe straps for fastening each pipe stake to the baseboard. Secure fastening here is essential. Use 10 x 1½-inch round-head wood screws to fasten clamps in place.)

### Finishing

If gable framing, baseboard, and lath material are made of redwood, give them two coats of redwood preservative. If other wood is used, treat with 2 percent copper napthenate. When wood is dry, you can follow up with two coats of exterior paint, color of your choice. Painting redwood is optional, of course. For more information on painting, see Chapter III. The galvanized pipe bows and other galvanized materials do not require additional finishing. (Note: Although all wood parts are not in place, it is a good idea to give protective treatment now. Later, some of the surfaces will be difficult to treat.)

### Covering

**XI-14.**   Using pliers or wire cutters, cut three 20 foot strips and one 10 foot strip of 4 x 4-inch

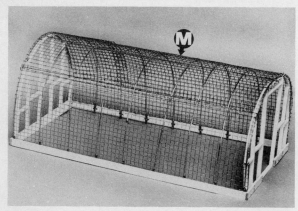

*XI-14*

12-gauge galvanized wire mesh M 72 inches wide. Now cut the 10 foot strip into two 3 foot strips. Using wire ties, cut from 14-gauge galvanized wire and spaced about 2 feet apart, fasten wire mesh M lengthwise onto top side of pipe bows. Be sure wire mesh is stretched reasonably tight.

*XI-15*

**XI-15.**   Cut 20 foot wide clear polyethylene 21 feet long; lay it aside for use as top covering later. Select a calm day for this step. Next, cut pieces of polyethylene N for the gable framework, fastening them in place with laths nailed to baseboard (see arrow) and studs with 4-penny box nails, spacing them about 10 inches apart. Leave lath-width space at top of framework for top laths to be fastened later. Be sure to cut out for doorway and ventilating fan assembly, if you intend to install one inside gable framework. Now, cover the pipe bows with single sheet of polyethylene O. Stretch tightly, fastening bottom edges to baseboards with laths and 4-penny box nails about 10 inches apart. Leave approximately a 6-inch surplus of polyethylene along top edge of both end pipe bows. Fold these ends of surplus down over gable polyethylene, holding in place on top plate with laths and nails as before. Refer to section on Covering Materials, in Chapter III, for a covering more durable than polyethylene.

**XI-16.**   Generally, polyethylene has a way of flapping, which reduces its life. To hold the polyethylene down, thereby reducing both noise and drip caused by flapping, and increasing film life, stretch pieces of 1½ inch wide polypropylene tape P, spaced approximately 2½ feet apart over top. Staple or nail both ends of each strip to

*XI-16*

*XI-17*

baseboard on opposite sides of house. The tape is designed for reuse, and many greenhouse supply houses handle it. For instance, the National Greenhouse Company carries it in 300-foot rolls.

If you would like to eliminate drip and reduce heat loss, consider double glazing the plastic-covered greenhouse. This can be done easily and quickly if bows are either ¾- or 1-inch pipe. Simply clip on an inside layer of polyethylene to the bows, at approximately 2-foot intervals, with clips especially manufactured for the purpose.

**XI-17.** Complete greenhouse by installing door Q. For installation information, see section on Doors in Chapter III.

(Portable Greenhouse Note: If wind becomes a problem, drive a wood stake at each corner with approximately one foot extending above grade. If extremely high winds are experienced in the area, drill a $\frac{5}{16}$-inch hole through stakes and baseboard. Then run a ¼-inch carriage bolt through each hole, followed by a washer and wing nut to hold stakes tight against baseboard.)

For plumbing, electrical, heating, ventilating, cooling, and humidifying equipment, as well as benches and other furnishings, see appropriate sections in Part I.

# XII

# Lean-to Model

**XII-1.** Now you can have that greenhouse you've always dreamed about. This model requires a minimum of effort and expense, yet it is durable, soundly constructed, and designed for the hobbyist. It has charm, as well as merits that'll bring great enjoyment to everyone who uses it.

Whether your pleasure is found in raising rare flowers or providing fresh vegetables and herbs for the family table, this is the greenhouse to provide the utmost in relaxation when you take time "to get away from it all."

This greenhouse includes an adequately sized door, 72 square feet of bench room within a floor area of approximately 108 square feet, and a natural ventilating system second to none. Power cross ventilation is possible without detracting from or changing the design. Double glazing, the newest trend in greenhouse construction to cut down on heating bills, is used and is fully explained.

Since the greenhouse walls and roof are of modular construction, it is a comparatively simple matter to increase or decrease the original dimensions. If you keep in mind the standard modules

*XII-1*

102

as original size is altered, no changes in construction techniques are necessary. All you do is increase or decrease the recommended materials proportionately.

Tools used for layout, making footings and foundations are found in Chapter IV. Other tools required are a drill and bits to suit, carpenter's hammer, saw, plane, and level, screwdriver, adjustable wrench, and paint brush. The glossary provides a definition and/or use of each.

Although redwood or cypress, which have high natural resistance to decay, are ideal for building the framework, they are sometimes not available. In this case, treat the available lumber with 2 percent copper naphthenate wood preservative.

A single glazed greenhouse has only one piece of glazing material, such as glass, fastened to each glazing frame, while a double glazed greenhouse has two pieces of glazing material fastened to each glazing frame. The following table lists material for building a single glazed Lean-To Greenhouse: 8 feet 10 inches x 11 feet 8 inches:

### Lean-To Greenhouse

| Parts | Description |
| --- | --- |
| Foundation A and footing | Concrete or concrete blocks for foundation Amount to suit* |
| Machine bolts | 10 ½ x 10 inches, washers and nuts |
| Scrap 2 x 4 | 2 pieces 2 x 4s (approximately) x 20 inches |
| Plates B | 1 piece 2 x 6 x 12 feet<br>1 piece 2 x 6 x 16 feet |
| Wall studs C | 1 piece 2 x 4 x 18 feet |
| Top plate D | 1 piece 2 x 4 x 12 feet |
| Wall studs E | 1 piece 2 x 4 x 14 feet |
| Top plate F | 1 piece 2 x 8 x 12 feet |
| End rafters G | 2 pieces 2 x 4 x 10 feet |
| Door frame H | 1 piece 2 x 4 x 16 feet |
| End studs I | 1 piece 2 x 4 x 10 feet |
| Door header J and wall rails K and L | 1 piece 2 x 4 x 18 feet |
| Cellar sash headers M, purlin N, and short rafter O | 1 piece 2 x 4 x 12 feet<br>1 piece 2 x 4 x 10 feet |
| Rafters P | 1 piece 2 x 4 x 18 feet |
| Purlins Q | 1 piece 2 x 4 x 12 feet |
| Glazing frames R | 1 piece 1 x 2 x 12 feet<br>2 pieces 1 x 2 x 10 feet |
| Glazing frames S | ½ x ¾ inch x 46 lineal feet |
| Corner trim T | 2 pieces 1 x 2 x 7 feet |
| Glazing frames U and UA | ½ x ¾ inch x 195 lineal feet |

| Parts | Description |
| --- | --- |
| Hotbed sash V | 2 pieces 3 x 6 feet |
| Hinges W | 5 pairs 3 x 3-inch fast-pin, rust-resistant butt |
| Sash adjusters X | 8 pieces heavy-weight pipe-strap 12 inches<br>16 round-head wood screws to suit<br>8 iron washers to suit |
| Cellar sash Y | 2 pieces 1 foot 8 inches x 2 feet 10 inches |
| Roof glazing material | 70 square feet of plexiglass |
| Side wall glazing material | 90 square feet of double-strength window glass |
| Glazing points | Number to suit |
| Door assembly Z | Door—type and size to suit<br>1 pair 3 x 3-inch hinges (unless already installed to door unit)<br>Door lock to suit (unless already installed to door unit)<br>2—⅜ x 1⅜-inches x 10-feet door stop and 14 4-penny finish nails |
| 2 percent copper naphthenate and paint<br>or | Amounts and color of paint to suit |
| Redwood stain for redwood frame | Amount to suit |
| Waterproof glue | Amount to suit |
| Caulking | Amount to suit |
| Nails | Approx. 1¾ lbs. 16-penny box |
| Nails | Approx. 2 ozs. 8-penny box |
| Nails | 4 1-inch galvanized |
| Nails | Approx. ½ lb 4-penny box |

* Depth, width, and thickness of footings and foundations vary so much from job to job that even an approximate amount of material, such as cement, sand, gravel, and concrete blocks cannot be given with any degree of accuracy.

Select a desirable site next to a building such as your home. In addition to points to consider in locating a site discussed in Part I of this book, give careful thought to locating the structure so doors or windows are not blocked, unless you want to provide access or share heat with the house. Here are two additional thoughts on location: 1. Including a basement window in the model allows furnace heat to be utilized in the greenhouse. 2. Taking in an outside hose valve located in the house foundation provides a convenient water supply. On the other hand, it is not a big job to install a freeze-proof outside hose valve through the house foundation, where it is connected to the cold water line in the basement or crawl space. See Chapter V for installation suggestions.

### Assembling

*XII-2*

**XII-2.**  Site layout, footing, and foundation are constructed next. For these construction details, see Chapter IV. Although this greenhouse can be built on the ground without footing or foundation, it is not recommended for two reasons: 1. Frost lines—if they occur in the area—will cause the structure to shift during winter weather, resulting in glass breakage as well as breaking apart of the greenhouse frame itself. 2. Frequently, the aesthetic value of the greenhouse and the attached building is lost, unless both structures have foundations similar in material and height. An attached building with a wall of the same materials from ground level up, such as brick or stone, would be the exception. Here the greenhouse could be constructed on a foundation (extending slightly above ground level) which rests on a concrete footing.

The picture shows poured concrete foundation A 2 feet high x 8 inches wide; it rests on a footing 16 inches wide. 10 ½ x 10-inch machine bolts (heads down) were placed vertically 1¾ inches from the outside edge of the foundation (not the form material) in the wet concrete as it was being poured. 2¼ inches (thread end) were allowed to extend above the foundation for later bolting down the framework plate. Exact spacing of the bolts in the foundation is not significant. The important thing is that they must not be placed in the foundation so that they are located under wall stud spacings. The actual door opening in the foundation was 3 feet (width of door) plus 3 inches (thickness of two 2 x 4 door frames) plus ³⁄₁₆ inch (space for door clearance), making a total width of 3 feet 3³⁄₁₆ inches. Scrap piece of 2 x 4 (shown by arrow) was nailed to inside of form at both ends of door opening to serve as a nailer for the 2 x 4 door frames—to be installed later. Outside edge of scrap pieces were placed within 2 inches from outside edge of foundation. To build a concrete block foundation (optional), use concrete grout material, as described in Chapter IV, to hold the bolts permanently in place inside the block voids. When 2 x 4 door frame is installed later, use ⅜-inch lag bolts and masonry anchors to fasten it to the block foundation.

*XII-3*

**XII-3.**  Now it is time to begin side wall framing. If you feel a bit shaky about carpentry work, see the section titled Woodworking Hints in Chapter III. Select straight stock for bottom plates B from one 2 x 6 x 16 feet and one 2 x 6 x 12 feet. Check ends that will adjoin house with a square; cut four plates B so they will extend 2 inches over side of foundation and will fit flush with inside of door opening in foundation. Be sure to cut ends of plates (see arrow) so they fit at 45° angles. (Note: If you are familiar with this kind of carpentry work, you can save time by combining Step 4 with Step 3.)

Next locate position of anchor bolt holes on the four plates. Place each 2 x 6 plate, one at a time, in exact position along side bolts in foundation. Using a square held against side of bolt, mark locations of bolts in their respective positions on plates, remembering that plates extend 2 inches beyond outside foundation edge. Then drill holes in plates about ⅛ inch larger than bolt size. Position plates over bolts and check for fit, making adjustments if necessary.

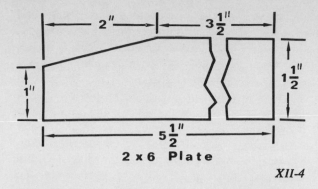

*XII-4*

**XII-4.** Remove plates from foundation. Using a plane, bevel outside edges as shown in the drawing. (Note: Keep 3½ dimension "full" as shown so it can later accept square end of wall stud.) The purpose of the bevel edge is to shed water away from the walls.

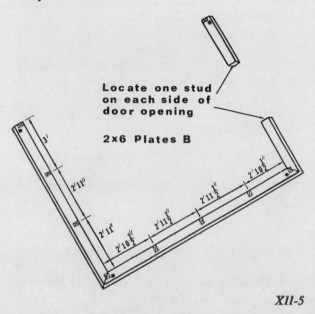

Locate one stud on each side of door opening

2 x 6 Plates B

*XII-5*

**XII-5.** Locate lower plates B on flat surface as they belong on foundation. Then layout and mark with an X wall stud locations as indicated in the picture. Arrows point to 2-inch space (distance plate overhangs foundation) between front plate edge and corner wall stud marking.

**XII-6, 7 and 8.** Cut five 2 x 4 wall studs C 3 feet 6 inches long and one 2 x 4 top plate D 11 feet 8 inches long (distance between outside edges of outer wall stud markings on plate). Next cut two 2 x 4 rear wall studs 7 feet long, followed by cutting 2 x 8 rear, top plate F same length as front, top plate. Make end lap joints on one end of rear

studs and at each end of rear, top plate F. Check joints for fit.

Place front, top plate D along side bottom plate B. Then mark stud locations on face of top plate. Mark same dimensions on top side of top plate to indicate rafter locations.

Now fasten front, top plate D to the five wall studs C, using two 16-penny box nails driven through face of plate into end grain of studs. Next fasten front, bottom plate B in same manner but only to the three middle studs. Bottom ends of end studs C are fastened in place later. Using same nailing procedure, fasten right and left, end bottom plates B to the two 7-foot rear studs, being sure end lap joint is topside and facing forward.

From this point on, a helper comes in handy. Position, one at a time, right and left end plates B with holes over bolts, making nuts finger-tight Using a 16-penny box nail fasten rear studs to adjoining building temporarily, position them perpendicular with a level. Nail rear, top plate F temporarily in position, being sure lap joints fit together at each end.

Position and fasten bottom, front plate B onto foundation, make nuts finger-tight. Next toenail bottom ends of end studs C onto bottom plate B, using two 16-penny box nails for each fastening. Temporarily nail braces (shown by arrow) to both adjoining front corner studs C and to their respective bottom plates B as noted.

Now make final line up of framework constructed thus far. Drive bottom plates B tightly in position on top of foundation with a hammer, being certain front miters fit together and that plates extend 2 inches over outside of foundation. Check with a carpenter's level that plates are

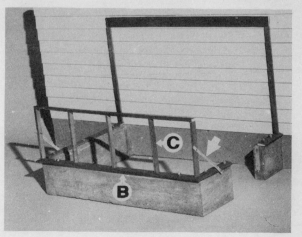

*XII-6*

horizontal. If not, shim with thin pieces of wood until they are level. With washers in place, tighten nuts with a wrench. Fill space, if any, with concrete grout mixed as described in Chapter IV.

Recheck studs C and rear studs with a level, they must be perpendicular before proceeding. Fasten rear studs as well as rear, top plate F, permanently in place. Space 16-penny box nails about 16 inches apart, drive them through stud faces into wall of adjoining building. Use four 8-penny box nails at each lap joint. If adjoining wall is masonry, use ¼-inch lag bolts and anchors instead of nails to fasten in place.

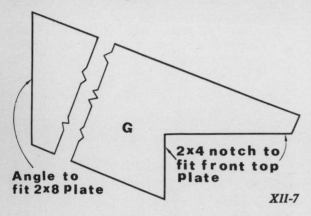

**Angle to fit 2x8 Plate**

G

**2x4 notch to fit front top Plate**

*XII-7*

Scale drawing is a guide for cutting rafters G in steps to follow. For transfer of angles from printed page to wood stock, refer to Chapter X, Figure 14.

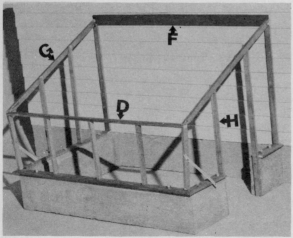

*XII-8*

Using picture in previous step as a guide, mark both angles on a piece of rafter material with an overall length of approximately 9 feet 2 inches. Saw rafter angle to fit against rear top plate F. Holding 2 x 4 rafter G in place against rear,

top plate F, check angle marking against top, front plate D. (Note: Because of slight variations in framing, due to variables such as sawing wastes, material warp, plumbness of adjoining building, etc., it is good practice from this point on to check all markings on lumber against actual construction before sawing to size.) With rafter G marked to fit, cut with saw. Check against location. Follow by checking on opposite side of framework, then cut duplicate rafter. Position end rafters G with front edge flush with bottom edge of rear, top plate F. Using two 16-penny box nails, one on each side, toenail end rafters G in place.

Frame end walls next. Cut two 2 x 4 frame studs H next, sawing stud notches to fit past rafters G on inside face. Use rafter angle as a guide. Check with level to be sure studs H are plumb, then fasten each stud, with two 16-penny box nails, to 2 x 4 nailer previously set inside of door opening in foundation. Fasten upper end of each stud H to 2 x 4 rafter G with two 8-penny box nails. Measure, mark, cut, and fasten in place two 2 x 4 left end studs, evenly spaced, toenailed to lower plate with one 16-penny box nail on each side and fastened to rafter, as done previously for door frame studs H.

*XII-9*

**XII-9.** Cut and fasten, with 16-penny box nails, door header J in place with clearance of 6 feet 8³⁄₁₆ inches between it and bottom of door entrance. Next cut and fasten in place 2 x 4 solid bridging pieces K and L. Here the idea is to frame them on same plane as front, top plate. Now cut and fasten cellar sash headers M in place with a clearance of 1 foot 8¼ inches. Later, two 1-foot 8-inch x 2-foot 10-inch cellar sash are installed to provide ventilation.

16-penny box nails) midway between purlin N and top plate D.

Remove the two temporary corner braces previously installed.

*XII-10*

**XII-10.** Cut 2 x 4 purlin N. Then transfer rafter markings to it from front, top plate D. Nail in place with 2-feet 10½-inches clearance between purlin N and rear, top plate F. Next cut and nail in place short rafter O 5 feet 10 inches on center from outside edge of either 2 x 4 end rafter G. Using angle cuts illustrated previously, measure, mark, cut and fasten three remaining 2 x 4 roof rafters P to their respective rafter markings on purlin N and top front plate D. Next cut to size four pieces of 2 x 4 purlins Q, fastening in place (with

**XII-11.** Cut two end glazing frames R from 1 x 2-inch stock, making overall lengths and angle cuts at each end to conform with adjoining end rafters G. Position 1 x 2s R onto and ½ inch above end rafters G with waterproof glue. Fasten in place with 6-penny box nails spaced approximately 16 inches apart. (Note: The projection above end rafter G is necessary to allow space for glazing a roof covering such as plexiglass.)

Next cut front glazing frame R from 1 x 2-inch stock so it is same length as front top plate. Bevel one edge with plane to conform with slope or angle of rafters. With bevel side up and flush with top edge of rafters, fasten in place the same as the end glazing frames.

Next make rafter-top glazing frame S ½ x ¾-inch stock. Cut two long pieces S to fit face down and snug between end glazing frames R. Then position one piece onto center of purlin N, the other on center of purlins Q. Fasten in place with waterproof glue and 4-penny box nails spaced about 16 inches apart. Cut in-between pieces to fit center and top side of rafters P and short rafter O as shown. Fasten in place the same as other rafter-top glazing frames.

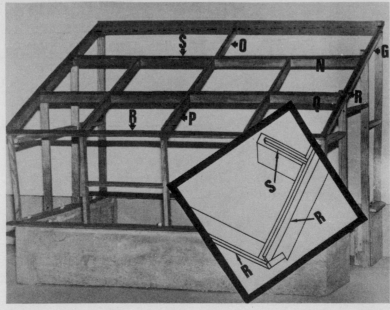

*XII-11*

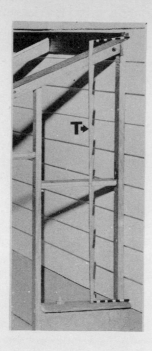

*XII-12*

**XII-12.** If adjoining building wall is masonry, skip this step. On the other hand, if it is siding, as in the picture, or other kind of uneven material, make a finish job by scribing a 1 x 2-inch corner piece T to adjoining wall at each of the two corners. Space 4-penny box nails 16 inches apart and fasten each one tightly to corner stud E.

**XII-13.** Next prepare wall framing for glaz-ing material. Rip ½-inch stock into strips ¾ inch wide. With exception of door opening and window sash openings, cut and position strips U ½ inch inside frame opening; fasten together with waterproof glue and 4-penny box nails spaced about 16 inches apart. You can make a neat job by mitering the corners (45°). (Note: ½-inch quarter round or window stop can be substituted.) When fastened to middle of studs, the ¾-inch strips leave ample space on either side for glazing, creating an ideal situation for double glazing now or later. The saving of heat pays for the extra glazing in a matter of a few years. Double glazing requires an additional 2 x 4 corner post at each of the two front corners: use pieces of ½-inch stripping between the two 2 x 4s and fasten together with 16-penny box nails staggered and spaced 16 inches apart. Each corner post is now 3½ inches thick to correspond with dimensions of remaining studs.

Use same material for stripping and fastening wall sash openings. The only difference is in positioning stripping UA inside openings. Here leave a space of ⁵⁄₄ inches (thickness of sash).

If you want to double glaze the roof, use ½-inch quarter round or window stop set in ½ inch on lower face of roof framing with exception of roof sash openings. No stripping is required here. To double glaze sash, simply staple plastic sheeting to the lower framework, leaving the plexiglass or glass exposed to the weather.

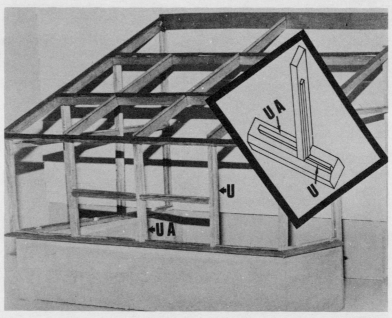

*XII-13*

## FINISHING

Examine the framework carefully, noting cracks, knot holes, and unfilled nail holes. Use a caulking gun to fill large knot holes and cracks and a glazing compound, or other wood filler, to fill smaller holes.

If framework is redwood, give it two coats of redwood preservative to retain its natural beauty. For other woods, treat with 2 percent copper naphthenate. Follow up with two coats of quality exterior paint to all framing and moldings before installing the plexiglass or glass and hotbed and cellar sashes, which should also be treated and painted prior to installation. Painting of redwood is optional, of course. For further information on painting see Chapter III.

## COVERING

### Ventilating And Cooling Sash

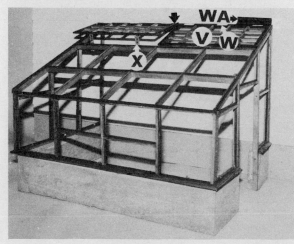

*XII-14*

**XII-14.** Position two 3 x 6-foot hotbed sashes V against rear, top plate and on top of glazing frames. Since sash ends should fit flush with end glazing frames, trim one end of each sash to fit. Bevel one side frame of each to fit snug against rear, top plate. Hold each sash in place with three 3 x 3-inch fast-pin, rust-resistant butt hinges W, fastened in place with accompanying flathead screws. Be sure sashes have ⅛ inch clearance between them. Weatherstrip (shown by arrow) by fastening a piece of ½ x 2-inch lumber, to one hotbed sash only, and in position as shown with 4-penny box finish nails. Position a single inch strip of plastic film WA lengthwise across hinged edge of hotbed sash to keep water out. Use screen molding WB or narrow strips of ½-inch lumber and 1-inch galvanized nails to fasten plastic strip to sash frame and house wall. Since shading is not involved here, use black polyethylene instead of white. The sun does not affect its life as readily as white. Mylar is even better for longer life. Prepaint molding before applying. For easy application, do it before covering roof structure.

Ventilating slide adjusters X can be purchased or parts bought cheaply from a hardware store and made at home. Cut a 12-inch length from heavy, perforated pipe strap. This material comes in straight pieces. Do not use the role type. Bend strap about 1 inch from one end in the form of an L. Using a roundhead wood screw with head larger than strap holes and a washer, fasten L end of strap loosely about 6 inches from each end of sash, as shown. Now fasten a roundhead wood screw, head slightly smaller than strap holes, ¾ of the way to inside of rafter header so it will be directly below adjusted arm. When sash is raised to desired height, slip strap over screw head. Alternately, fasten a piece of chain in place to keep sash from opening too far. This is particularly important if sash is subject to high winds.

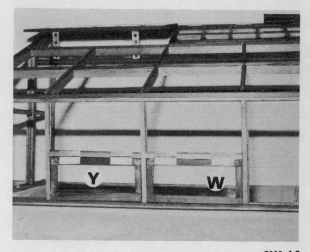

*XII-15*

**XII-15.** Position two 1-foot 8-inches x 2-feet 10-inches cellar sash Y in place as noted. If they fit tightly, plane edges. Using hinges and ventilating adjusters make installation similar to hotbed storm sash installed previously. W and X are explained in Step 14.

**Glazing**

Many glazing materials are on the market today for use in greenhouse construction: plexiglass, plate glass, double-strength window glass, and Mylar, to mention a few. Check with local greenhouse supply houses to find out what material is best for long wear, in terms of cost, for your locality. For average conditions, I recommend plexiglass for the roof covering and double-strength window glass for side wall coverings. Both materials can be obtained from lumberyards. Measure each opening, with exception of sash and door openings, as you make a list of number of pieces and sizes required for each. For proper fit, record each piece ⅛ inch smaller than respective opening. Regardless of type of glazing material selected, install roof first. With hotbed sashes propped open against adjoining building wall, begin glazing operation with an opening near roof middle, filling in openings from here toward ends. For installation, see section entitled Glazing in Chapter III.

**XII-16.** Several installation possibilities of door Z are shown in Chapter IV.

*XII-16*

It is possible to have power ventilating and cooling in conjunction with the movable sash system installed. This is an important consideration if the climate is extremely hot.

# XIII

# Sunglow-Lite Model

**XIII-1.** The Sunglow-Lite is for a beginner learning greenhouse gardening from the ground up, or a professional with many years of experience in commercial hothouses. Clear walls from eave to bottom plate doubles the growing space, since plants thrive both below and above bench level. The rigid structure is built on a wood sill, which is bolted securely onto a foundation of short poles set in the ground—poured concrete or concrete blocks. All wood, including pole foundation, is treated with a nontoxic preserva-

tive. Hand-operated vents for ventilating and cooling control are provided to conserve on energy during warm weather. Back-up power vents can be installed for extremely hot, muggy weather.

If careful workmanship in cutting and assembling is a rule of the day rather than an exception, a sturdy frame will be the result. Although this model has tremendous expansion and covering possibilities, always space the framework according to the required width and kind of covering. For example, space the frames on 32-inch centers

*XIII-1*

for 34-inch wide corrugated fiberglass, and on no more than 36-inch centers for vinyl or polyethylene. The shatterproof, hailproof model illustrated here has frames spaced on 36-inch centers for accepting flat sheets of clear fiberglass 36 inches wide. Although framings increase in size from the 18-foot width to the 27-foot width, the rafter angle cuts, both at ridge and eave, remain the same. The techniques recommended here can be used also to build a gable-type, lean-to greenhouse where the wall of an adjoining building is substituted for the end wall without a door.

Tools used for layout, making footings and foundations are given in Chapter IV. Other tools necessary to build this freestanding greenhouse are a drill with bits to suit, carpenter's hammer, saw and level, screwdriver, adjustable wrench, and household stepladder. The glossary provides definition and/or use of each.

Use construction grade lumber or better, and treat it for durability with 2 percent copper naphthenate. Eliminate potential problems in hard-to-get-to-places by treating the lumber before it is assembled. Redwood or cypress both have natural resistance to decay and lend themselves readily to sawing and shaping.

The following table lists materials for building a 12 x 15-foot freestanding greenhouse. Heating and ventilating are easy to control in this size. To construct a greenhouse wider than 12 feet, note that as widths increase, framing lumber widths also increase: from 2 x 4s to 2 x 6s. To use covering other than 36 inches in width, it is necessary to respace the framework to suit covering requirements.

## Freestanding Greenhouse

| Parts | Description | Parts | Description |
|---|---|---|---|
| Footing and/or foundation A | Concrete, concrete blocks, or wood poles | Sash adjusters | 8 assemblies:<br>8 pieces heavy pipe strap 12 inches<br>8 washers<br>16 round-head wood screws |
| Machine bolts | Fifteen ½ x 10 inches with washers and nuts | | |
| Bottom plates B | 2 pieces 2 x 4s x 16 feet<br>1 piece 2 x 4 x 10 feet<br>1 piece 2 x 4 x 12 feet | Caulking | Amount to meet requirements |
| Wall studs C | 6 pieces 2 x 4s x 12 feet | Closure strips P | 1 piece 1 x 2 x 16 feet |
| Top plates D | 2 pieces 2 x 4s x 16 feet | Flat sheet fiberglass covering | 36 inches long x 490 lineal feet |
| Rafters E | 6 pieces 2 x 4s x 14 feet | | |
| Ridge board F | 1 piece 2 x 6 x 16 feet | Glazing strips | ½ x 1½ inch x 400 lineal feet |
| Front and rear gable-wall studs G | 2 pieces 2 x 4s x 8 feet<br>1 piece 2 x 4 x 9 feet<br>4 pieces 2 x 4s x 14 feet<br>2 pieces 2 x 4s x 12 feet | Door assembly Q | 1—3 x 6 feet 8 inches<br>1 pair of hinges, type to suit<br>1 lock set or latch to suit<br>18 lineal feet of doorstop |
| Door frame header H and wall rails I | 2 pieces 2 x 4s x 16 feet<br>2 pieces 2 x 4s x 12 feet | | |
| Wall headers J and Roof purlins K and L | 4 pieces 2 x 4s x 12 feet | Paint | Quantity depends upon type and condition of wood and brand of paint used. See instructions on container |
| Corner braces M | 4 pieces 2 x 4s x 10 feet | | |
| Wood strips or door stop for Cellar sash stop | 2 pieces ½ x 1½ x 10 feet | | |
| Hotbed sash N | 2 pieces 3 x 6 feet | Nails | Approx. 6 lbs. 16-penny box |
| Cellar sash O | 2 pieces 1 foot 8 inches x 2 feet 10 inches | Nails | Approx. 2 ozs. 8-penny box |
| Hinges | 5 pairs 3 x 3-inch fast-pin, rust-resistant butt | Nails | Approx. 2 ozs. 4-penny box |
| | | Nails | Approx. 1 lb. 1½-inch galvanized |

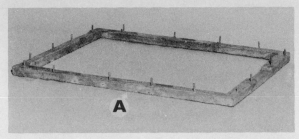

XIII-2

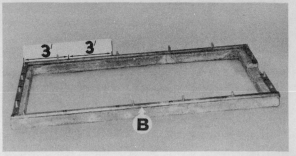

XIII-4

**XIII-2.** Chapter IV tells how to construct foundations of poured concrete, concrete blocks, or poles. Bring the one that suits your requirements approximately 5 inches above grade. Foundation A shown in the picture is of poured concrete with 17½ x 10-inches plate-mounting, machine bolts, spaced approximately 42 inches apart and 1¾ inches from outside edge. Locate a bolt near both sides of each corner, as well as near each end of the door opening. Check with steps to follow so bolts are not placed under wall studs (erected later).

## ASSEMBLING

XIII-3

**XIII-3.** Wall framing comes next. Before starting, see section titled Woodworking Suggestions in Chapter III. Select straight stock. Then cut two bottom plates B from 2 x 4s 15 feet long to fit top sides from end to end of foundation, one 2 x 4 11 feet 5 inches long to fit between them at rear of foundation, and two 2 x 4s to fit front of foundation, fitting flush at door opening. Butt joints should make a good fit.

Placing each 2 x 4 plate, one at a time, along side anchor bolts, mark locations for drilling holes. Make holes approximately ⅛ inch larger than diameters of bolts. Position bottom plates over bolts and check for fit, making adjustments if necessary.

**XIII-4.** With double stud marking X placed at each corner, (as shown on one wall of founda-

tion) layout remaining stud locations on plates B 3 feet on centers, beginning at outside edge of corner studs. There is one exception on the door opening end. For a 3 foot wide x 6 foot 8 inches high door, locate these stud markings 3 feet from outside stud edge of corner stud to center marking of first stud, second stud 18 inches on center, third stud flush with door opening. This completes one half of door opening wall stud locations. Complete wall stud marking on remaining half of plate on door opening end of foundation in the same way as for the first half.

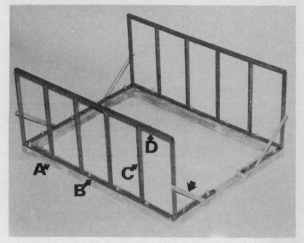

XIII-5

**XIII-5.** Cut twelve 2 x 4 x 6-feet wall studs C and two 2 x 4 top plates D exactly the same length as corresponding bottom plates B. Then position top plates D along side bottom plates B. Mark stud locations so that spacing on both plates are exactly the same. Fasten top and bottom plates onto wall studs by using two 16-penny box nails driven through face of plates into end grain of studs.

Although this can be a one-man job, a helper makes the work easier and swifter. I have found two men working together can do as much work as three men working independently. Position both wall stud frames over foundation bolts. With washers in place tighten nuts finger-tight. Be sure outside edges of bottom plates B are flush with outside foundation wall A. Next position end, bottom plates B over foundation and between side, bottom plates, tightening nuts finger-tight. With bottom plates B in perfect alignment, wrench-tighten nuts. Plumb wall studs with a level, holding them in position by nailing scrap pieces of lumber (shown by arrow) to them and end, bottom plates as noted.

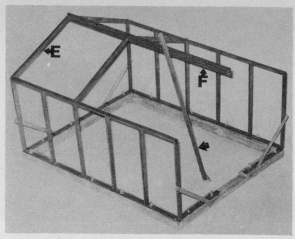

*XIII-7*

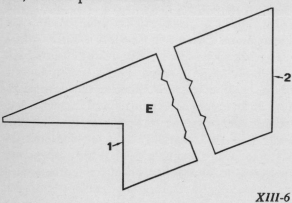

*XIII-6*

**XIII-6.** Cutting rafters is next. The scale-size drawing serves as a guide for cutting rafters E in the following steps. The first shows bottom cut (notch), while the second shows top cut or cut fitting against roof ridge plate. Suggestions for the transfer of angles from printed page to wood stock are given in Chapter X, Figure 14. (Note: Rafters extend ¾ inch over top plate.)

**XIII-7.** Using picture above as a guide, make rafter E from straight 2 x 4 stock. Saw top cut and bottom notch, making overall length 6 feet 6½ inches. With this piece as a pattern, cut identical rafter. Next cut ridgeboard F 15 feet long (check against length of top plates) from 2 x 6 stock. Positioning ridgeboard F along side one of the top plates, transfer stud markings. (Note: Later, rafters are to be fastened to top plates directly over stud locations.)

Before proceeding, check pair of rafters for proper fit. With lower ends (tails) temporarily nailed to bottom plates, one rafter directly across from the other, and a scrap piece of 2 x 6 held between top cuts, rafter joint should be equal distance from each bottom plate. When rafters make a good fit, remove temporary nails. Then

mark one piece with a P to serve as a rafter pattern. Cut five more pairs of rafters E from 2 x 4 stock.

Using two 16-penny box nails, fasten one end of ridgeboard F to top end of rafter E, being sure ridgeboard extends 1¾ inches above top edge of rafter (thickness of hotbed sash plus ½-inch glazing strips to be installed later).

Nail a second rafter E on the same side of ridgeboard D but two or three rafter positions away. Have helper—working from stepladder or scaffold—raise the ridgeboard with the two rafters as you position each notched end of the rafters over the X markings on top plate. Fasten in place with a 16-penny box nail on each side to toenail rafter to top plate. Next nail in place two rafters E opposite the first two. Using a 16-penny box nail on each side of top rafter end, toenail to ridgeboard F. Plumb and brace this part of the rafter framework by temporarily nailing a 2 x 4 brace (shown by arrow) to ridgeboard and stake driven in ground as noted. Now complete rafter E assembly.

Check final plumb on rafter framework with a level, readjusting 2 x 4 brace if needed. *Caution:* 2 x 4s for rafters and wall studs work satisfactorily on widths up to 15 feet. For widths from 18-27 feet, use 2 x 6s for both wall studs and roof rafters. Increasing only greenhouse lengths has no effect on either wall stud or rafter widths (see Figure 9).

**XIII-8.** Remove the four pieces of scrap lumber braces from corner studs and bottom plates. Then cut front and rear gable-wall studs G. Two corner studs and four additional studs make up

*XIII-8*

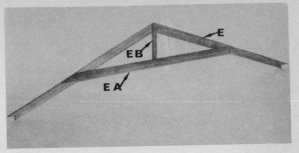

*XIII-9*

the front end framing with two middle ones doubling as a door frame. Two corner studs and three additional studs make up the rear end framing.

With the exception of the corner studs, which are same length as side wall studs, saw notches on top ends of remaining studs to fit past rafter E on inside face (Figure 6 is guide for making angle cuts). Plumbing studs, use two 16-penny box nails to toenail lower end of studs to bottom plate. Also, use two 8-penny box nails to fasten upper end of each notched stud to 2 x 4 rafter E. Using 16-penny box nails spaced on 16-inch centers, fasten end wall corner studs to side wall corner studs.

Be sure to remove 2 x 4 temporary brace from ridgeboard.

**XIII-9.** The following two steps are required only if the model described in this chapter is widened and lengthened. Otherwise, proceed to Figure 10. First, if greenhouse is to be wider than 12 feet, add roof purlins so the spacing remains approximately three feet apart. Also, expand ventilating openings accordingly. Prepare more door frames if more than one door is required. In order

to increase the width from 15 feet to 27 feet, the addition of support assemblies is necessary, each consisting of a 2 x 6 pair of rafters E, a 2 x 6 collar beam EA, and a 2 x 4 brace EB as noted. For purposes of clarity, only a single set of 2 x 6 rafters E with attached assembly are shown. (Note: Collar beam assemblies need only be attached to every other pair of roof rafters.) Second, if greenhouse is to be longer than 15 feet, more support is required than just those at the end gables. For example, a 4 x 4-inch center post treated with nontoxic preservative is recommended for a greenhouse 18 feet long. Set one end on a footing. Dig a hole (with a post hole digger) about 6 inches below frost line. Nail four pieces of scrap lumber, or use upper part of a gallon can to bring the hole approximately 6 inches above grade. As you pour hole and form full of concrete, insert two flat pieces of strap iron ½ x 2 x 16 inches long approximately 10 inches in the concrete, so the 4 x 4 support post will fit snug between them. Let the concrete set for 48 hours. Then drill two ½-inch holes opposite each other in the strap iron pieces. (Note: If you work accurately, it is easier to drill the holes prior to placing them in concrete.) Position support post between strap iron pieces. Toenail top end of post to ridgeboard with 16-penny box nails. Next drill ½-inch holes through bottom of post, using holes in strap iron as guide holes. Run ½ x 6-inch machine bolts through the holes followed by washers and nuts fastened wrench-tight. This model lends itself ready to a 100-foot length. However, the longer the greenhouse is made, the more supports are required; space them approximately 9 feet apart. (Note: If your greenhouse requires collar beam assemblies, as mentioned above, locate the support posts so the collars can be nailed to them with 16-penny box nails. This step gives added support to the structure.)

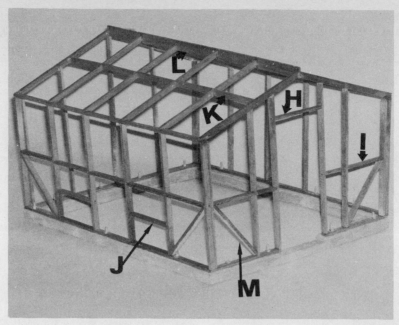

XIII-10

**XIII-10.** Saw door frame header H from a piece of 2 x 4. Then fasten in place 6 feet 8¾₁₆ inches above bottom of door framing using two 16-penny box nails driven through face of each 2 x 4 door frame into end grain of header. If your plans call for an exhaust fan with shutters, you have plenty of room to frame a 2 x 4 opening to fit between door frame header H and gable roof rafters. (Note: For clarity, framing pieces in this step are shown in the picture only on one side of roof, one side of side wall, one side of end wall.)

Next, measure and cut 17 wall rails I from 2 x 4 stock to fit between wall studs with exception of door opening. Then position the wall rails midway between top and bottom plates, fastening in place with 16-penny box nails.

The framing for cool air wall vent J is next. Measure and cut two 2 x 4 headers J. Fasten them in place 1 foot 8¼ inches above bottom plate as noted with two 16-penny box nails driven through face of wall stud into end grain of header. This provides frames for later mounting two cellar sashes 1 foot 8 inches x 2 feet 10 inches.

There are two rows of roof purlins K and L on each roof slope. Measure and cut 16 pieces of 2 x 4 stock to fit between roof rafters as noted. Position lower face of purlin K parallel to and 3 feet from 2 x 6 ridgeboard F. Fasten in place with 16-penny box nails in the same way as wall rails

were fastened. Position and fasten purlins L adjoining ridgeboard. Where roof ventilators are installed, only one purlin L is required. This is located between hotbed sash locations adjoining ridgeboard F.

This step is optional for the size of greenhouse illustrated, unless the area is subject to high winds. Install two corner braces M at each corner for larger greenhouses. Braces are from 2 x 4 stock mitered at ends to fit flat against bottom plate and corner wall stud. Position on bottom plate and corner wall stud. Then fasten in place with two 16-penny box nails driven through face of brace at each end.

Fasten ½-inch x ¾-inch wood strips, ½ x ½-inch quarter round, or window stop—mitered at ends—in place with 4-penny finishing nails ⅝ inches back from lower wall cellar sash openings, countersink the heads. Fill holes with glazing compound or wood filler.

## FINISHING

Fill any large cracks and knotholes with a caulking gun. Glazing compound or wood filler can be used for small cracks and nail holes.

Redwood retains its natural beauty if it is treated with redwood preservative; it can, of course, be painted. Treat other woods with 2 percent copper naphthenate if they are untreated at this point of construction. Give framework two quality coats of exterior paint, color of your choice. Additional suggestions on painting are given in Chapter III.

## COVERING

### Ventilating and Cooling Sash

**XIII-11.** Roof ventilators N are made with two hotbed sashes 3 x 6 feet.

*XIII-11*

Bevel one edge of sashes N so they will fit snug against ridgeboard. Position them against ridgeboard with several pieces of glazing strips (used later for holding roof covering in place) temporarily placed between bottoms of sashes N and roof rafters. Fasten three 3 x 3-inch fast-pin, rust-resistant butt hinges to each sash N and ridgeboard, as noted. Refer to Chapter XII, Figure 14, for applying plastic weatherproof strip to hinged edge of roof ventilators.

Regulate opening and closing of sashes with ventilating slide adjusters, two to each sash. These can be purchased from your local lumberyard or you can make them, see Chapter XII, Figure 14.

*XIII-12*

**XIII-12.** Position two cellar sashes O 1 foot 8 inches X 2 feet 10 inches inside the frames formed by wall studs and 2 x 4 headers. Fasten each sash in place with a pair of hinges similar to those used above for fastening the hotbed sashes in place. Sash adjusters are installed in the same manner as the hotbed sashes above.

### Glazing

Filon flat sheet fiberglass covering was used in the model illustrated because it is reputedly shatterproof and can withstand vibration, shock, and hail. Many greenhouse and building supply dealers carry it. For instance, Peter Reimuller—Greenhouseman, Santa Cruz, California lists Filon flat sheet stock in four-ounce weight, in rolls 25 feet long, 36 inches wide. Check size before making purchase.

Double glazing greenhouses pays for the cost by saving energy. Refer to Chapter XII, Figure 13, for an easy way to glaze the inside greenhouse walls and roof.

*XIII-13*

**XIII-13.** Before applying flat sheet fiberglass, make closure strips P by ripping 1 x 2 stock diagonally. Then cut 10 pieces to fit between lower end of rafters and top plate. Nail in place with 4-penny nails, countersinking heads. A continuous surface should exist between lower rafter surface and face of closure strips. Use a plane to make strips conform to rafter pitch if necessary. I prefer to plane closure strips before installation. However, if finishing nails are countersunk sufficiently, the job may be easier once the closure strips are fastened in place.

Install Filon roof sheets, beginning at the end that makes your work easier as you proceed to the opposite end of the roof. Cut lengths required to run from ridgeboard, or roof ventilators as the case might be, to eave with about ¾ inch extending over lower edge of top plate. 36-inch widths cover one rafter-to-rafter space. Position sheets, holding in place with molding or ½-inch lumber ripped into 1½-inch strips and 1½-inch galvanized nails spaced about 12 inches apart. Seal the joints of the flat fiberglass sheets over center of rafters, against ridgeboard, and roof ventilator frames with a caulk seal prior to fastening molding strips in place, for better waterproofing of the roof. Nail molding strips as you work, since it is difficult to put them on later without roof scaffolding as a support. Remember too, prepainting molding strips makes it necessary to give only a touch-up coat as they are installed. Complete glazing operation by cutting and installing Filon fiberglass strips onto wall studs; follow suggestions, above, for glazing the roof. Flat fiberglass sheets should extend from lower edge of bottom plate to top edge of top plate, fitting snug against overhanging roof sheets.

## ALTERNATIVE COVERING METHOD ONE

Some greenhouse builders prefer to glaze with corrugated Filon fiberglass panels. If this is the choice, space the framing to accommodate available widths, which can be purchased from most greenhouse supply houses, some lumberyards, and a few mail-order houses. Be sure to obtain fiberglass designed especially for greenhouses. At the time of purchase, obtain the accessories described below. Cut the panels as the flat fiberglass sheets above were cut.

The panel corrugations run parallel to the roof rafters and wall studs. Fasten panels in place with 1¾-inch x 10-gauge aluminum nails with neophrene washers. Use horizontal 2½-inch corrugated polyfoam molding to close corrugations on top of top plate at upper end of panels. Both polyfoam molding and aluminum nails can be obtained from the suppliers of fiberglass panels.

## ALTERNATIVE COVERING METHOD TWO

Sometimes it is more realistic, from a budgetary point of view, to glaze with a cheaper, plastic material than those described above. A more permanent material can be applied at a later date. If a substitute glazing material is used, be sure the frames can accommodate the widths before they are purchased. Many, many different kinds of plastic materials are on the market. Here are just a few that are installed in a similar manner over the greenhouse framework; they can be purchased from most greenhouse supply houses. Polyethylene comes in rolls up to 14 feet in width and from 1-10 mils thick. It has a relatively short life, usually anywhere from a few months to a year. Vinyl film comes in thicknesses ranging from 3-12 mils and is available in sheets 4-6 feet in width. It has a life expectancy of between two and four years. Mylar polyester comes in 4-6-ounce weights and is available in widths of 28 inches; the life expectancy is between three and five years. Generally, the longer the life of a plastic the more it costs. Before making purchase, check price against life expectancy with the supplier.

*XIII-14*

Once the material is selected, measure and cut the lengths required to run all the way over the roof from lower edge of bottom plate on one side to bottom of lower plate on the opposite side. Staple at one bottom plate, then stretch tight and staple to other bottom plate. Rather than staple from one end of plate to opposite end, it is a better idea to center covering. Then staple from center of plate to each end. Next position and nail molding or lattice strips with 1½-inch galvanized nails. In this way you can work each way with plenty of room to get the plastic sheeting stretched and fastened in place as you go. (Note: Stretch and strip down plastic around roof ventilators as you work. Once a vent opening is held permanently in place, cut out sheeting inside vent frames.) Apply the plastic sheeting to the wall area in the same manner.

**XIII-14.** Several ways of door installation Q are described in Chapter III.

For plumbing, electrical, heating, power ventilating and cooling, and humidifying equipment, as well as benches and other furnishings, see appropriate sections in Part I.

# Appendix

**TABLE I.   Concrete Mixes and Their Functions**

| Proportions of Materials* | | Type of mixture | Where used |
|---|---|---|---|
| From Ready-mix** | Use when mixing concrete yourself | | |
| 6 bag | 1-1½-3 | High stress | Driveways, roads, columns |
| 5 bag | 1-2-4 | Standard | Sidewalks, arches, roofs, beams, foundations, footings |

\* The first figure stands for cement, the second sand, and the third refers to the number of parts of stone or gravel. A bag of cement contains one cubic foot. Thoroughly mix the dry ingredients. Then mix again, using enough clean water, free of alkali, acids, or other foreign matter, to form a completely plastic and workable concrete.

\*\* Specify either five bag or six bag mix. The company takes care of properly mixing the correct amounts of sand and rock.

**TABLE II. Lumber Sizes**

| Specification sizes | Actual dimensions | Specification sizes | Actual dimensions |
|---|---|---|---|
| 1 x 2 | ¾ x 1½ | 2 x 8 | 1½ x 7¼ |
| 1 x 3 | ¾ x 2½ | 2 x 10 | 1½ x 9¼ |
| 1 x 4 | ¾ x 3½ | 2 x 12 | 1½ x 11¼ |
| 1 x 6 | ¾ x 5½ | | |
| 1 x 8 | ¾ x 7¼ | | |
| 1 x 10 | ¾ x 9¼ | | |
| 1 x 12 | ¾ x 11¼ | | |
| 2 x 2 | 1½ x 1½ | | |
| 2 x 3 | 1½ x 2½ | | |
| 2 x 4 | 1½ x 3½ | | |
| 2 x 6 | 1½ x 5½ | | |

(Note: Where 5⁄4 material is specified, its actual thickness is the same as specification size: 1⅛" or 5 quarters. The actual dimensions of finished lumber is less than specification size because of drying and planing. When placing orders, list the specification sizes and not the actual dimensions.)

## CORRESPONDENCE COURSES

If you want to learn more about greenhouse gardening but find it impractical to attend classes, don't be discouraged. Many greenhouse owners have profited by taking approved correspondence courses. It's almost like having an instructor looking over your shoulder. I recommend the following courses provided by The Pennsylvania State University, Correspondence Courses in Agriculture, 202 Agriculture Education Building, University Park, Pa. 16802:

1. *Plant Life.* A basic course for those who work with or are interested in plants. Their structure, water and mineral needs, nutrition, growth, reproduction, and breeding are discussed briefly. How plants live, develop, and reproduce, how they vary in structure and form, how crop plants are improved, how we make use of plants and plant products, and many other topics are included. 10 lessons, 8 Study Points, Cost $5.50, Rewritten 1970 by M. H. Runner.

11. *Propagation of Plants.* Plant propagation is the basis of two industries in agriculture: the nursery and the seed production businesses. This course presents a comprehensive discussion of 1. seed production including genetics, breeding, and seed processing; 2. seed sowing and transplanting of seedlings; 3. vegetative propagation including cuttage, division and separation, layerage, grafting, and budding; and 4. nursery management. 10 Lessons, 15 Study Points, Cost $5.50, Revised 1972 by Chiko Haramaki.

139. *The Home Greenhouse.* A basic course to help the beginner and a review for the experienced hobby greenhouse operator. Instruction includes principles and practices in location, construction, heating and ventilation, and equipment for greenhouses. Plastic and sash greenhouses for temporary use are also discussed. One lesson is devoted to managing the greenhouse and another to a few favorite plant materials and their propagation. 6 Lessons, 5 Study Points, Cost $3.50. Revised 1972 by R. A. Aldrich.

## GREENHOUSE SUPPLIERS

Aluminum Greenhouses, Inc.
14615 Lorain Avenue
Cleveland, Ohio, 44111

Greenhouse Specialties Company
9849 Kimker Lane
St. Louis, Missouri, 63127

Hydroponics Industries, Inc.
Suite 236
Greenwood Plaza, Terrace Building
Englewood, Colorado, 80110

Ickes-Braun Glasshouses
P.O. Box 147
Deerfield, Illinois, 60015

Lord and Burnham
Irvington, New York, 10533
or
Des Plaines, Illinois, 60018

National Greenhouse Company
Pana, Illinois, 62557

Redfern's Prefab Greenhouse Manufacturing
Company
55 Mt. Hermon Road
Scotts Valley, California, 95060

Peter Reimuller—Greenhouseman
P.O. Box 2666
Santa Cruz, California, 95060

Sturdi-Built Manufacturing Company
11304 Southwest Boones Ferry Road
Portland, Oregon, 97219

Texas Greenhouse Company
2717 St. Louis Avenue
Fort Worth, Texas, 76110

## REFERENCES FOR GREENHOUSE GARDENERS

### Books

The following books contain simple basic information about the growing and caring of greenhouse plants, as well as other information related to the greenhouse:

Neal, Charles D., *Do-It-Yourself Housebuilding: Step-By-Step*, Macmillan Publishing Company, 866 Third Ave., New York, N.Y., 1973. A complete coverage of all aspects in building any kind of one-story wood building, particularly helpful to the gardener in building the office, store, garage, or furnace room in connection with the greenhouse. It is illustrated with over 600 pictures and is written in plain English.

Nelson, Kennard S., *Greenhouse Management for Flower and Plant Production*, The Interstate Printers and Publishers, Inc., Danville, Illinois, 1973. The information in this book is primarily for the commercial greenhouse foreman. However, the cultural aspects of greenhouse gardening—the soil environment and the air environment, as well as business procedures, engineering, and marketing—are equally important to the hobbyist.

Anonymous, *Electric Gardening*. Second Edition, Edison Electric Institute, 750 Third Ave., New York, N.Y., 1970. Although this book is for the hobbyist as well as the commercial gardener, it gives a rather broad and general discussion of the use of electricity in the greenhouse.

Field, Edwin M., *Oil Burners,* Second Edition, Theodore Audel and Company, Indianapolis, 1970. Actually the book covers much more than the title suggests. It treats everything related to oil burners, such as petroleum, heating systems, combustion, ignition systems, electrical wiring (including controls), pumps, blowers, oil storage, and maintenance.

Oravetz, Jules, Sr., *Plumbers and Pipe Fitters Library—Drainage, Fittings, Fixtures.* Theodore Audel and Company, Indianapolis, 1968. This book contains valuable information for the greenhouse gardener who wants to learn just about everything in the plumbing business that applies to the greenhouse. Particularly important are Chapter 1, "Water Supply," Chapter 5, "Pipe Fittings," and Chapter 7, "Valves and Faucets."

Palmer, M. L., et al., *Private Water Systems, Midwest Plan Service-14,* Cooperative Extension Service, Ohio State University, Columbus, 1968. An essential manual for the greenhouse gardener who must develop his own water source.

Ecke, Paul, Jr., and O. A. Matkin, *The Poinsettia Manual,* Paul Ecke Poinsettias, Encinitas, California, 1971. This manual is a complete discussion of poinsettia production, including recommendations on cropping.

Laurie, Alex, D. C. Kiplinger, and Kennard S. Kelson, *Commercial Flower Forcing,* Seventh Edition, McGraw-Hill Book Company, New York, N.Y., 1969. An excellent source of information on control of cropping for all major greenhouse flower and plant crops, including detailed pot plant rotation.

Mastalerz, John W., Robert W. Langhans, et al., *Roses—A Manual on the Culture, Management, Diseases, Insects, Economics, and Breeding of Greenhouse Roses,* Pennsylvania Flower Growers, University Park, New York State Flower Growers Association, Inc., Ithaca, 1969. In addition to the subjects mentioned in the title there is a short discussion on timing, pruning, and supporting.

Mastalerz, John W., and Robert W. Langhans, et al., *Roses—A Manual on the Culture, Management, Diseases, Insects, Economics, and Breeding of Greenhouse Roses,* Pennsylvania Flower Growers, University Park, New York State Flower Growers Association, Inc., Ithaca, 1969. This manual covers various aspects of soil management, including such topics as "growing Media, Soil Aeration, Soil Treatment,

Kohnke, Helmut, *Soil Physics,* McGraw-Hill Book Company, New York, N.Y., 1968. An excellent source for the gardener who is interested in understanding how science is involved in soil management. Although the title may suggest highly technical material, the book is actually easy to read and understand.

Water Requirements and Irrigation Practices, Fertilization, Mulches, Weed Control, Root and Stem Disease, Nematode Problems, and Soil Insects and Related Pests."

Pfahl, Peter B., *The Retail Florist Business,* Second Edition, The Interstate Printers and Publishers, Inc., Danville, Illinois, 1973. This book covers all phases of retail marketing of flowers and plants.

### Circular, Leaflets, and Pamphlets

The circulars listed below may be obtained from the Agricultural Publications Office, 123 Mumford Hall, Urbana, Illinois, 61801 (single copies free).

C793 Soil Sterilization Methods for the Indoor Gardener. 8 p.

C796 An Easy Method for Germinating Flower Seeds. 12 p.

C801 Flowering Gift Plants: Their Care and How to Rebloom Them. 56 p.

C817 Plant Breeding as a Hobby. 32 p.

C844 Hydroponics as a Hobby: Growing Plants Without Soil. 16 p.

C884 Growing Vegetable Transplants. 32 p.

C886 Plant Regulators—Their Use as a Hobby. 16 p.

C904 Geraniums for the Home and Garden. 16 p.

C930 Flowering Annuals for Sun and Shade. 16 p.

C980 Care of Flowering Potted Plants. 6 p.

C981 Growing Tomatoes at Home. 12 p.

C997 Gardening in Containers. 16 p.

C1036 Vegetables for Minigardens. 7 p.

Many other leaflets and pamphlets are available from the Department of Horticulture at other state universities. The following publications may be obtained from the Office of Information, U.S. Department of Agriculture, Washington, D.C., 20025.

G 67 Insects and Related Pests of House Plants: How to Control. 16 p.

G 80 Home Propagation of Ornamental Trees and Shrubs. 12 p.

G 82 Selecting and Growing House Plants. 32 p.

A B 237 Controlling Insects on Flowers. 80 p.

### Magazines

The following magazines are devoted to the interests of the greenhouse gardener:

*Plants Alive*
2100 North 45th Street
Seattle, Washington, 98103

*Under Glass*
P.O. Box 114
Irvington, N.Y., 10533

# Glossary of Greenhouse Terms

**Algae** Simple green plants known by the scientific name of *pleurococcus* or *protococcus*.

**Ampere** A unit used for measuring the rate of flow of electricity.

**Bar Tongue** The notch cut on a bar which is the frame into which glass panes are fastened.

**Batter Boards** Short, horizontal boards fastened to stakes driven in the ground and set in pairs forming a square at each corner of the building site just outside the building lines.

**Bond** The adhesion between two objects, such as two concrete blocks.

**Brick Set** A chisel-like tool used for cutting pieces of masonry, sometimes called a brick chisel.

**British Thermal Unit (BTU)** A unit of measure indicating the amount of heat required to raise the temperature of one pound of water one degree F.

**Building Code** A list of building trade rules and regulations designed for a specific community.

**Carpenter's Hammer** Sizes vary, but one weighing 16 ounces is generally used in the construction of greenhouses.

**Carpenter's Level** Consists of a rectangular body of metal or wood fitted with glass tubes partially filled with nonfreezing liquid, used for bringing various stages of construction to a vertical or horizontal position.

**Caulking Gun** A tool used to spread caulking material either from its own cylinder or from an attached tube.

**Circuit** Two or more wires through which electricity flows away from a source of supply to one or more pieces of equipment, such as a light, service outlet, motor, etc., and then returns.

**Circuit Breaker** A safety device which automatically breaks the flow of electricity whenever a circuit becomes overloaded.

**Closing Block** The last block laid in the middle of a course.

**Collar Beam** A board attached to each of a pair of rafters to keep them from spreading apart, thereby sagging under extra stress, such as snow.

**Conductor** An electrical term used to denote materials able to carry electricity.

**Convection** Transfer of heat in liquids and gases (air inside the greenhouse) by means of currents.

**Coupling** A plumbing fitting used to join two pipes.

**Course of Blocks** A specified number of blocks laid end-to-end forming a layer.

**Crosswebbs** Those divisions forming the inside cell walls of a concrete block.

**Deed Covenant** Building and construction regulations written into property deeds. They are intended to perpetuate the wishes and desires of the original owner.

**Double Edger** A small rectangular steel blade (fastened to a wood handle) with a depression along center on bottom side; it is used to form grooves across freshly poured concrete walks or driveways.

**Downspout** Pipe, generally fastened to outside wall, leading water from eave trough.

**Drill** A shaft-like tool, with two or more cutting edges, capable of making holes in construction materials when rotating at proper speeds.

**Eave** The horizontal part of the roof slope meeting the top of the vertical walls.

**Edger** A small rectangular steel blade (fastened to a wood handle) curved at a right angle on one side; it is used to give a professional look to edges of freshly poured concrete walks or driveways.

123

**Face Shells**   The outer portions of a concrete block.

**Facia Sash Frame Stock**   Used here to denote the face side of a board nailed over end rafters.

**Fish Tape**   A tape fastened to a reel and used to fish electric wires through conduit and walls.

**Flush Joint**   A joint level with a masonry surface.

**Footing**   A base on which a foundation rests.

**Foundation**   A prepared base built on top of a footing on which a building is constructed.

**Framing Square**   A steel square; the widest part—24 inches long—is called the body, and the narrowest part—16 inches long—is called the blade. Each section has measurements inscribed in fractions of inches.

**Gable**   That portion of a wall located directly under the slopes of a double-sloped roof.

**Gain**   A shallow rabbet for receiving the leaf of a butt hinge or half-surface butt hinge.

**Garden Hoe**   A long-handled tool having a thin, flat blade mounted transversely on one end of the handle.

**Garden Hose Valve**   A metal valve fastened to a water-supply line for the purpose of attaching a garden hose.

**Glazing**   Fastening glass or windows to a framework.

**Glazing Chisel**   A specially designed tool made of steel, used in conjunction with a carpenter's hammer for driving glazing points in wood framework, thereby holding glass panes firmly in place.

**Glazing Points**   Small pieces of sharpened steel pins that are used to hold glass in a framework of wood.

**Grounding**   A means of connecting the electric system to the earth.

**Grout**   A mortar generally made with sand and Portland cement mixed with water to a pancakelike batter. It is used for filling cracks and small holes in masonry.

**Gutter**   The part of a guttering system that catches rain water striking roof.

**Handsaw**   A thin metal blade with a series of sharp teeth. An 8 point is used for general crosscutting; an 11 or 12 point is used for finish work. Use a ripsaw for ripping boards.

**Horsepower**   One horsepower equals 746 watts.

**Hot Wire**   The electric wire carrying electricity, usually black or red.

**I.D.**   Inside diameter.

**Insulation**   A protective covering placed over wires to prevent escape of electricity.

**Jointer Tool**   A metal tool used for shaping joints in masonry work.

**Kerf**   A shallow cut made by a saw in a piece of wood.

**Knockout**   A round plate partially fastened to a metal electric box, such as a switch box, outlet box, or service panel cabinet, for easy removal to allow passing of wires into box.

**Layout**   An arrangement or plan of a complete building or any of its separate parts.

**Leveling Board**   A straight, unwarped board, 1 x 4 inches x 8 feet long, on top of which is placed a carpenter's level resulting in a check for levelness over an 8-foot distance rather than just the length of the level itself.

**Line Block**   A small, specially cut wood block positioned from outside two opposite corners of masonry for holding a stretched cord which serves as a guideline for the mason to lay concrete blocks, bricks, or stone in a straight, horizontal line.

**Line Level**   A miniature level, weighing about half an ounce. Although its use does not result in the same accuracy gained from using a transit, it is not as expensive as a transit or as costly as employing an engineer to do the leveling job. A line level plus a carpenter's level are sufficiently good instruments with which to lay out a greenhouse.

**Long-Nose Pliers**   Pincers with long, tapered jaws. They are used for holding small objects, bending wires, etc., in close quarters.

**Meter Box**   A metal box housing the electric meter.

**Miter**   An angle cut on a piece of wood to butt against an angular cut on a second piece of wood.

**Module**   A select unit of measure that is used as a basis for standardization of certain building materials.

**Multipurpose Tool**   An electrical tool used to cut and strip wire, attach terminals, and etc.

**Muntin**   Carpentry term used to denote a bar for holding the edges of window panes within the sash.

**Nail Set**   A tool used for driving heads of brads, casing nails, or finishing nails below wood surface.

**Neutral Wire**   The electric wire purposely grounded.

**Nipple**   A plumbing term referring to a short piece of pipe, usually between 2-8 inches long.

**Nonmetallic Cable**   Nonmetal material used for covering electric wires.

**Nylon Cord**   Made of nylon and used because it is nonstretch.

**O.D.**   Outside diameter.

**Outlet**   An electric device designed for tapping off electricity at specific locations for appliances and lights.

**Per Foot Run**   A run is the shortest horizontal distance covered by a common rafter. Per foot run refers to each lineal foot of run.

**Pipe Bender**   A metal tool used for bending pipe and conduit to some preconceived shape.

**Pipe Cap**   A plumbing fitting used at the end of a water supply pipe to terminate water flow.

**Plane**   A carpenter's tool fitted with an adjustable

steel blade, used for paring, truing, or smoothing wood.

**Plate** That piece of framework either on top or on bottom of studs, i.e., top plate or bottom plate.

**Plexiglass** (Trademark, Plexiglas) A lightweight thermoplastic polymer of methyl methacrylate. Because of its durability, and resistance to weathering, it is used in place of glass in many greenhouses.

**Pliers** Pincers with jaws, used for holding small objects, bending wires, etc.

**Plumb Bob** A metal weight with a point at one end and a hole for attaching a cord at the other end; it is used for establishing one point vertical with another point.

**Purlins** Solid framing members located between roof rafters.

**Rabbet Cut** A groove cut in one piece of material, such as wood, to receive a second piece of material, such as a sheet of glass in a greenhouse covering frame.

**Radiant Heat** Fin-type radiation heaters transfer heat energy by waves or straight lines similar to heat transferred by the sun. Such heat makes for a more closely related temperature between floor line and roof than that of heaters which transfer heat by convection currents.

**Rafter** Sloping timbers or metal pieces for supporting a roof.

**Rail** Carpentry term used for horizontal members in doors, windows, and furniture.

**Rake** The slope from the horizontal of a gable-type roof.

**Readi-Mix Concrete** A mixture of Portland cement, sand, rock, and water. (There are special trucks for hire that blend these materials enroute between source of supply and job site.)

**Receptacle** A type of outlet used for plugging in electric cords to a circuit.

**Reducer Bushing** A plumbing fitting designed to receive pipe of one diameter at one end and a pipe of another diameter at the opposite end.

**Ridge** The location where rafters of a roof meet at their uppermost ends.

**Run** An electrical term used to denote distance from box to box.

**Sash** A framework in which transparent materials, such as glass or plexiglass are set.

**Scissors** A cutting instrument consisting of two blades pivoted together, used for cutting soft materials such as polyethylene, paper, cloth, etc.

**Screwdriver** Tool used to tighten screws and locknuts where slotted bolt heads are used.

**Service Panel** The main panel through which electricity is brought from the power lines and then distributed to the various branch circuits in the electrical system.

**Shutoff Valve** A metal valve installed in a water-supply line for the purpose of cutting off supply when repairs are required.

**Sill** The bottom part of a greenhouse, resting horizontally and directly upon the foundation or wall.

**Single-Phase** An electric device, such as an electric motor, that is energized by a single electronic force with one phase or with phases differing by 180°.

**Steel Tape** Made of steel; it gives more accurate results than one made of cloth.

**Stile** Carpentry term used to denote the upright framing member in doors and windows.

**Storm Sewer** A sewer intended for rainfall disposal, not to be confused with a sanitary sewer (which should carry away sewage only).

**Strikeoff Board** Generally, a 2 x 4 used to level freshly poured concrete flush to the top of form.

**Stringers** A framework, such as the 2 x 4s fastened to posts in a board-on-board windbreak-type fence.

**Studs** Upright frame members, such as 2 x 4s, used in outside walls and partitions as part of the building frame.

**Temperature Relief Valve** A metal safety valve installed in top of hot water heater to relieve the pressure automatically if overheating occurs.

**Template** A pattern, generally made of heavy paper or a thin piece of metal or wood, used as a guide or an aid by craftsmen.

**Three-Phase** An electric device, such as an electric motor, that is energized by three electronic forces differing in phase by one third of a cycle or 120°.

**Toenail** To nail at an angle through one member into a second member.

**Trap** A plumbing fitting designed in the form of an S to allow waste fluids to pass into drain line and at the same time retain enough fluid to block sewer gas from entering the building.

**Tri-Square** A steel blade mounted at right angle to a face of metal or wood stock; it is used to "square" a board prior to sawing.

**Trowel** A concrete finisher's trowel that has a rectangular steel blade (fastened to a wood handle) and is used to produce a slick finish on freshly poured concrete; a bricklayer's trowel has a triangular steel blade (fastened to a wood handle) and is used to handle mortar during masonry work.

**U Bolt** A round bar of iron fitted with screw threads on both ends and bent in the form of the letter U, fitted with a double flat washer and two nuts.

**Vent Pipe** A pipe used in plumbing to release sewer gas to the outside above the roof as well as allow air to enter drain line, thus preventing waste fluids from being sucked out of trap.

**Vermiculite**   A group of platy minerals, magnesium, hydrous silicates of aluminum, and iron.

**Voltage Drop**   An electrical term used to indicate the voltage loss which occurs when wires in a circuit are overloaded.

**Wall Rails**   Solid framing members located between wall studs.

**Watt**   A unit used in electricity equal to the power produced by 1 ampere in a 1-volt circuit.

**Windbreak**   A growth of deciduous trees or evergreens, or a structure of boards, whose purpose is to shelter an object, such as a greenhouse, from severe wind blasts.

**Wood Chisel**   A tool made of steel, used for cutting or shaping wood; it has a cutting edge on one end and a handle on the opposite end.

**Wood Hand Float**   A rectangular wood tool used by concrete finishers to press down rock and to bring sand and cement to the surface of freshly poured concrete.

**Zoning Ordinance**   Special restrictions on the type of buildings that may be constructed in each of several areas or districts making up a town or city.

# Index